The Unofficial Cookbook for Your

All American® Pressure Canner

120 Foolproof and Fun Recipes for Home Preserving

by
Sandra May

The Unofficial Cookbook for Your All American® Pressure Canner: 120 Foolproof and Fun Recipes for Home Preserving

Copyright ©2018 Sandra May

Cover photo credit:
annabieniek / Depositphotos.com
Back cover: Shusha /Depositphotos.com, akulamatiau /Depositphotos.com spline_x /Depositphotos.com, sarahdoow /Depositphotos.com

All interior photos are from Depositphotos.com: p. 19 anna.pustynnikova, p. 54 bhofack2, p. 95 rlat28, p. 106 zkruger, p. 115 phloenphoto, p. 137 zoryanchik, p. 155 akulamatiau, p. 167 spline_x, p. 180 Shusha, p. 198 HandmadePicture, p. 213 sarahdoow

All rights reserved.
The use of any part of this publication reproduced, transmitted in any form or by any means, electronic, mechanical, recording or otherwise, or stored in a retrieval system, without the prior consent of the publisher is an infringement of the copyright law. In the case of photocopying or other reprographic copying of the material, a license must be obtained before proceeding.

All American® is the registered trademark of National All American Industries, Inc. home of world famous All American® Pressure Cookers, Pressure Canners and innovative Electric Appliances.

Legal Disclaimer
The information contained in this book is the opinion of the author and is based on the author's personal experience and observations. The author does not assume liability whatsoever for the use of or inability to use any or all information contained in this book, and accepts no responsibility for any loss or damages of any kind that may be incurred by the reader as a result of actions arising from the use of information in this book. Use this information at your own risk. The author reserves the right to make any changes he or she deems necessary to future versions of the publication to ensure its accuracy.

INTRODUCTION

Why Is This Introduction So Important?

Pressure canning at home is a bit like ballroom dancing in high heels: if done right, it's totally awesome – a consistent crowd-pleaser, the perfect marriage of art and science, the envy of all who behold it; but done wrong, it is a messy embarrassment at best, and a dangerous catastrophe at worst.

Now, I get it – I tend to be the type who skims my way through furniture-assembly instructions, or skips the guidelines and manuals entirely for cooking appliances, figuring I can just learn as I go and get things right eventually. And, for most cooking appliances and other devices, that method works just fine. But getting the full use of a pressure canner in your own home is not like using most appliances and devices – pressure canners are powerful tools, and if misused they can bring serious risks.

I'm not issuing this advice to try to dampen anyone's enthusiasm for pressure canning or home-preserving in general. On the contrary – this is precisely the advice I was given when I began my own adventures in pressure canning years ago: read all the instructions, heed all the safety advice, don't skip the manuals. I did just that – and still do – and I've never been sorry!

Getting it right is not particularly hard or complicated – but it does require the patience and focus to thoroughly read all guidance provided and available, including but not limited to this recipe-book introduction. As long as you don't cut corners and equip yourself with all the recommended knowledge, your home pressure-canning adventures will be safe and delicious every time!

Pressure Canning vs. Everything Else

Forget the old-time notions of water-bath canning – those are the unwieldy contraptions that your grandmother may have had going anytime someone wanted to take a hot shower; a lot of effort and time for a few jars of the same old jams and preserves that (let's face it) we can only eat so much of.

Those traditional home-preserving methods are only good for high-acid foods – think your typical fruit jellies and conserves. These methods are simply not suited to canning much else than peaches and strawberries, due to the chemistry involved in the preserving process. Namely, because these methods do not exert enough sustained hot pressure to kill botulism and other food-borne illness that could be present in low-acid foods like meat or vegetables.

That leaves out an awful lot of food groups, and literally infinite delicious meals that you can't preserve at home. Of course, you could go to the grocery store and buy ready-made cans or jars of just about any meal you can imagine. But store-bought goods are rarely going to be as delicious as what you make with love right in your own kitchen – not to mention the fact that they're too often laden with preservatives, additives and other suspect chemicals. Those mass-produced canned products simply can't compare with the sense of well-being that comes with knowing exactly what goes into every bite of your family's meals.

Enter the pressure-canning method, which takes that world of the preserving-possible and expands it by multiples. These devices are custom-designed to withstand high and sustained hot pressure to perfectly preserve anything from nutrient-rich vegetables to protein-packed meats and fish. Want to put up a jar of your absolute favorite meaty pasta sauce, to have ready in minutes flat at the end of some busy day months or even years into the future? A pressure-canner is what you need, and oh how delicious it will be.

I've been pressure-canning everything from steak to bouillabaisse for a few years now, and this book of recipes is the result of everything I've learned through this exciting – and delicious – adventure. I know there was life before I got my pressure canner, not to mention some pretty good meals. I just can't remember what it was like – and I now can't imagine life without my homemade pressure-canned goodness!

Caution! What NOT to Put in Your Pressure Canner

As I've gushed above, the modern pressure-canner is a truly marvelous device – almost magic. But not *quite*.

There are some food groups that it simply cannot support, most importantly large amounts of fat, oil and grease (which can wind up "climbing" the jars and interfering with the proper sealing of the lids, which means your food is not properly protected from disease agents), as well as any low-acid foods that naturally contain high amounts of fat (even foods we don't typically think of as "fattening," such as dairy products).

It's also wise to generally keep flour and other thickeners out of your pressure-canned jars, since it's difficult to predict exactly how they'll react under the hot pressure – safer just to steer clear, as do all the recipes in this book.

The list of foods whose pressure-canning safety cannot be guaranteed includes but is not limited to:

- Milk
- Cream
- Cheese
- Bacon
- Butter
- Lard
- Eggs (including pickled eggs)
- Refried beans (regular beans are fine)

- Cake

- Flour

- Cornstarch

- Bread

I realize that to dairy- and BLT-lovers this might seem like a daunting list, but trust me, once you get going you'll discover that there's literally no end to the awesome recipes you can make in your pressure-canner. And hey – the lower fat diet will not only be delicious and super convenient, it might just be good for your health as well!

Know Your Altitude! The Importance of Pressure

You'll notice that all the recipes in this book offer adjusted pressure settings depending on how far above sea level you are. Do not ignore these instructions! It's very important to adjust your pressure-canning according to your elevation, since the atmospheric pressure and its effects on your processing do change the further up you get from sea-level.

So whatever you do, don't guess and don't skip this step. Before you begin any canning project check the altitude of your location. In the age of the internet, it's not hard to find a website to let you know your exact altitude – from VeloRoutes, to the aptly named WhatIsMyElevation.com or Altitude.org, call your local information services and they should be able to help.

What's in a Gauge? (Weighted vs. Dial)

The recipes in this book are all spelled out for weighted-gauge pressure canners, which I strongly prefer over dial-gauge canners due to their ease of use and the added safety redundancies inherent in the design. There are some well-reputed dial-gauge pressure canners on the market, but I'll be honest and admit that my experience with them is limited, and this recipe book is strongly tailored for use with weighted-gauge models.

If you are using a using a dial-gauge canner for these recipes, be sure to double-check the applicable instructions in the users' manual that came with the product, and to adjust the pressure settings listed in these recipes accordingly. This is pressure canning, after all – so the pressure is important to get right!

How to Use This Book:

This book is loosely organized by ingredient category, so readers can easily find whatever type of dish they want. Every recipe includes full set-up and processing instructions, along with safety and clean-up steps, so there's no need to read them in any order – feel free to skip around.

Cooks should *not* attempt to use or adapt any of the meat, fish or vegetable recipes in this book for use with a water-bath or other canning method. As stated above, the pressure canner is the *only* safe way to preserve these foods, and there is simply no way to ensure the safety of your products using other canning methods.

The recipes in this book are all measured for maximum use of a 21.5-quart weighted-gauge pressure canner. Needless to say, cooks may well want to prepare smaller amounts, and in all cases can adjust the measurements accordingly.

As with all culinary adventures, cooks should be aware of any relevant allergies and avoid using any ingredients that might provoke an adverse reaction.

Which Pressure-Canner Is the Right Pressure-Canner?

I've already stated my strong preference for weighted-gauge models of pressure canners, both for their user-friendliness and for the built-in safety advantages. Any well-made weighted-gauge pressure canner should be fine for all these recipes and more. That said, the only model I can personally recommend is the All-American® 921 model, since it's the only model I've personally used for every single recipe in this book.

There's a reason for that, too; I did plenty of research before taking the leap into pressure canning, and the All-American® product is quite simply the best on the market, by far. The price tag is on the higher end, but trust me when I say that it's more than worth the added value in quality and durability. Built with hand-cast aluminum and a unique metal-to-metal system of sealing for ultra-secure processing, the All-American® is as well-made as it gets.

The metal-to-metal sealing system also means the All-American® pressure canner has no need for gaskets – truly a godsend when it comes to cleanup! It's just a bonus that this sleek design also makes it exceptionally attractive; this is one large kitchen appliance you'll be proud to have out when friends pop by.

Best of all are the safety features in the All-American® 921 model, which include a geared steam gauge and an overpressure pipe that releases automatically. The weighted-gauge pressure settings are foolproof, and All-American's customer service is second to none.

Finally, as the name promises, the 921 pressure-canner is 100% made in the good old US of A! If you're serious about investing in home preserving using the best of the best materials, this is the only pressure-canner worth your time and money.

Storage and Labeling Tips

Every recipe in this book, if prepared and processed correctly, will preserve nutritional content of the foods for a minimum of three years – and often much longer. It's important, however, to always store your sealed jars in a cool, dry place, and generally safe from accidents or jostling. Never use contents in jars whose lids have been dented, and always check to make sure that the food looks and smells good before serving.

In all cases, it's a very good idea to label your jars the day after processing, once they are fully cooled and ready for storage. Write down the date – day, month, and year – of the canning, and also write down the ingredients or name of the dish (jars can come to look indistinguishable, and you're better off not making yourself guess), along with any preparation or serving notes that you want to include.

As noted in the recipes – but important enough to stress here! – examine all your jars after processing. You'll know that your lids did not seal correctly if they can be pushed down afterwards; this happens from time to time, and when it does you should either reprocess the contents, or refrigerate them and serve within 2-3 days.

A Brief Word on Pickles, Pickling, and Veggies in General

Readers may notice that this recipe does *not* include its own section for pickles and pickling recipes. Most canning books do, but for pressure-canning books, pickle recipes are pure filler.

The fact is that, as popular as pickling is, you don't need a pressure-canner to do it – regular boiling water and brine will do – and indeed pickling is in most cases not appropriate for canning under pressure. A well-made weighted-gauge canner can, however, be easily modified for such use, by opening the pressure valve and following regular boiling-water pickling methods. I use my All-American® in this way all the time, and it works great! I particularly recommend it for home-pickling beets and, of course, pickles!

The section for vegetarian dishes in this book is for all those wonderful meals that you can't preserve any other way – the nutrient-packed, fresh-flavorful jars of asparagus soup, savory vegetable stews, and the pantries stocked with fresh-canned leafy greens from kale to collards. These are the vegetable dishes that will keep your family rosy-cheeked throughout the winter, prepared and jarred up right in your own home, preserving all the goodness that you can't buy at the grocery store.

Ultimate Super Safety Advice

This recipe book and the instructions throughout are intended as guidelines. In all cases, readers should carefully read and follow the specific instructions and user manuals included with their pressure canner, as products differ in their suitability and usage.

It's important to be well acquainted with the various parts of any kitchen device you're using, and particularly when it comes to your pressure canner. Readers will note that every recipe here includes pre-preparation instructions to check the state of their pressure canners before use – this step is absolutely crucial, as are the follow-up steps for clean-up and proper maintenance.

Where any instructions in this book differ with the manufacturer instructions included with the pressure canner, always defer to the manufacturer instructions. And, if in doubt, there are multiple public agencies available to advise on the scientifically tested methods for home preservation.

The U.S. Department of Health and Human Services operates FoodSafety.gov, which provides a wide range of resources for home canning, and specific guidance for pressure canning. The U.S. Department of Food and Agriculture also offers a wide range of resources online, including the "Complete Guide to Home Canning" available free on the web, and can be contacted by phone at +1 (202) 720-2600.

Finally, never forget the cardinal basics of home-preserving safety: Never leave your pressure unattended while in use, always check the look and smell of your jarred foods before serving, and don't skip any safety steps or instructions. Pressure canning is a fun and practical way to preserve all your family's favorite dishes; put safety first and keep your common-sense wits about you, and there will be sumptuous feasts to follow!

TABLE OF CONTENTS

SOUPS, STEWS, & CHILI 19
    Down South Soup Starter 20
    Northern Garden Vegetable Soup Starter 22
    Butternut Squash Soup Base 24
    Chicken Corn Chowder Base 25
    Clam Chowder Soup Base 27
    Vegetable Broth 28
    Smooth and Easy Fennel and Carrot Soup 30
    16 Bean Soup 32
    Beans and Salsa Soup 34
    Chicken Garbanzo Soup 35
    Layered Chicken Soup 36
    Italian Meatball Soup 38
    French Onion Soup 40
    Potato and Leek Soup 41
    "Hoowee!" Chili 43
    Mushroom Cap Soup 45
    Tomato and Roasted Red Pepper Soup 47
    Condensed Tomato Soup (using Clear Jel) 49
    German Beef Stew 51
    Chili Con Carne 53

MEATS & MAIN DISHES 55
    Sausage and Peppers 56
    Corned Beef Hash 58
    Chicken and Vegetable All-Purpose Head-Start 59

- Almost Done Beef Stroganoff ... 61
- Spaghetti Sauce with Ground Venison ... 63
- Chicken, Corn and Lentil Spring Mix ... 64
- Asian Turkey Meatballs ... 67
- Chicken Meatballs ... 69
- Beef Bourguignon ... 71
- Chicken Pot Pie Filling ... 73
- Sweet and Sour Chicken ... 75
- Mushroom, Spinach and Chicken Medley ... 77
- Chicken Cacciatore ... 79
- Pulled Pork ... 81
- Apple Butter Pork ... 82
- Rascally Rabbit ... 84
- Turkey Sausage ... 85
- Chicken ... 87
- Lemon Salmon in Vinaigrette ... 88
- Garlic Lemon Trout ... 89
- Tuna ... 91
- Salmon ... 92
- Garlic Mushroom Chicken in Tomato Sauce ... 93
- Sloppy Joes ... 94
- Taco Meat ... 96

BEAN RECIPES ... 98
- Summer BBQ Beans ... 99
- Back Home Pork and Beans ... 101
- Ranch Style Beans ... 103
- Boston Baked Beans ... 105

    Kidney Beans 107

SALSA 109

    Tomatillo Green Salsa 110

    Black Bean and Corn Salsa 111

    Peach Salsa 113

    Pineapple Mango Salsa 115

    Spicy Salsa 116

JELLIES, JAMS, & MARMALADES 118

    Country Meadow Dandelion Jelly 119

    Cabernet Wine Jelly 121

    Jalapeño Jelly 122

    Pepper Jelly 123

    Carrot Jam 125

    Banana-Orange Jam 126

    Apricot Mango Jam 128

    Blackberry Jam 129

    Pina Colada Jam 131

    Rhubarb Conserve 132

    Strawberry Lemon Marmalade 134

    Citrus Trifecta Marmalade 135

    Blueberry Orange Marmalade 137

    Blood Orange Marmalade 138

SPREADS, CHUTNEY, & RELISHES 140

    Apricot Honey Butter 141

    Paw Paw Butter 142

    Roasted Red Pepper Spread 143

    Pear-Persimmon Chutney 144

- Rhubarb Chutney 146
- Tomato Rhubarb Chutney 148
- Corn Relish 150
- Zucchini Relish 152
- Chow-Chow 154
- Ikra 156

CONDIMENTS & SYRUPS 158
- Teriyaki Sauce 159
- Tomato Ketchup 160
- Provencal Tomato Sauce 162
- Spicy Barbecue Sauce 164
- Pecan Syrup 166
- Blueberry Syrup 168

PICKLED VEGETABLES 170
- Sweet Pickles 171
- Fairy Tale Eggplant Pickles 172
- Green Tomato Pickles 174
- Pickled Figs 176
- Cowboy Candy (Sweet Pickled Jalapeños) 178
- Pickled Baby Artichokes 180
- Spiced Pickled Beets 181

CANNED VEGETABLES 183
- Home Canned Soup Vegetables 184
- Roast Tomatoes 186
- Sliced Green Tomatoes 187
- Marinated Mushrooms 188
- Glazed Carrots 190

- Green Beans 191
- Herbed Peas 192
- Corn 193
- Mexican Style Corn 194
- Chard, Collards, and Kale 195
- Garlic Dill Zucchini 196
- Sweet Potatoes 198
- Candied Yams 199

JUICES & FRUITS 201
- Strawberry Pineapple Lemonade Concentrate 202
- Pina Colada Concentrate 203
- Fruit Salad 204
- Honey Blood Orange Slices 206
- Candied Kumquats 208
- Maraschino Cherries 209
- Spiced Pears 210
- Port and Cinnamon Plums 212
- Honey-Bourbon Pickled Blueberries 214

DESSERTS & DELICACIES 216
- Pecan Pie Filling 217
- Cherry Pie Filling 218
- Spiced Apple Pie Filling 220
- Mincemeat Pie Filling 222
- Southeastern Green Tomato Mincemeat 224

1

SOUPS, STEWS, & CHILI

DOWN SOUTH SOUP STARTER

Convenience food doesn't have to be the chemical-laden, nutritionally lacking options taking up far too much space on the nation's supermarket shelves. Canning your own nourishing, healthy whole foods gives you the best of both worlds — the convenience the pace of modern life sometimes demands and real food you can trust. This soup starter features classic southern garden vegetables, giving you a good start on a healthy pot of soup for a delicious, fast dinner. This recipe makes about 7 quarts.

INGREDIENTS:

- 2 gallons tomatoes
- 16 ears of corn
- 6 small onions
- 4 hot peppers
- 2 cups green lima beans
- 1 ½ cups chopped okra
- 1 cup sugar
- ½ cup salt
- 1 cup vinegar

DIRECTIONS:

1. Drop the tomatoes a few at a time in a pot of boiling water, leaving them in for 15 seconds, just long enough for their skins to slip off easily. After all the tomatoes are peeled, chop them.
2. Cut the corn off the cobs, then finely chop the onions and peppers.
3. In a large, heavy stainless steel pot, combine tomatoes, corn, onions, peppers, lima beans, okra, sugar, salt and vinegar. Put the pot over

medium-high heat. When the pot comes to a full, rolling boil, reduce the heat to medium and boil for 30 minutes.

4. While the pot is boiling, get your All American® pressure canner set up and ready to process. Sterilize 7 quart jars and lids. Leave them in simmering, not boiling, water until you are ready to fill them.

5. When the pot has boiled for half an hour, turn off the heat and ladle the hot vegetable mixture into hot jars, allowing 1 inch of headspace. Use a chopstick or long, slim plastic spatula to break up any air bubbles or pockets.

6. Wipe jar rims and threads carefully with a clean, lint-free damp cloth, making sure that there is no residue or any food particles that could interfere with the jar sealing properly. Put the lids and rings on the jars, then carefully lower them into the pressure canner.

7. Process the jars for 85 minutes at 10 pounds of pressure. After following depressurization and venting procedures, remove jars from canner and set on a towel to cool undisturbed for at least 12 hours. After 12 hours, you can check the seals on the jars.

8. Store securely sealed jars in a cool, dark place for up to 12 months. If a jar fails to seal well, store it in the refrigerator and use its contents within 3 or 4 days.

Northern Garden Vegetable Soup Starter

Soups offer healthy, economical, convenient meals. Having a selection of home canned soups and soup starters on your pantry shelves will help keep you and your family well fed and well nourished, even when busy days leave little time for cooking. This soup starter features vegetables that folks north of the Mason-Dixon line would think of as traditional, basic soup ingredients. From this time-tested foundation, great soups are built. This recipe makes between 4 and 5 quarts or between 8 and 10 pints.

INGREDIENTS:

- 1 quart chopped celery
- 1 quart chopped onions
- 6 chopped green peppers
- 4 quarts ripe, peeled and chopped tomatoes
- 1 quart water
- 3 tbsp. salt
- 2 tbsp. sugar

DIRECTIONS:

1. Put all of the ingredients in a large, heavy stainless steel pot over medium heat and simmer for 20 minutes.
2. While the vegetables are simmering, prepare the All American® pressure canner for processing. Sterilize the necessary number of jars and lids. Leave the sterile canning equipment in simmering water until needed.
3. Fill the hot jars with the hot soup starter. Wipe the jar rims and threads carefully with a damp paper towel or cloth, removing any food particles or residue that could interfere with the sealing process. Put hot lids on the jars and tighten the rings. Lower the jars into the

pressure canner and process pints at 10 pounds of pressure for 25 minutes and quarts for 30 minutes, also at 10 pounds of pressure.

4. After depressurizing and venting the pressure canner, transfer the jars to a towel spread on a table, a section of the counter or a shelf where they can sit, undisturbed, for at least 12 hours. After that time, you can check the seals on the jars.

5. You can store securely sealed jars for up to 1 year in a cool, dark spot. If a jar didn't seal completely, put it in the refrigerator and use its contents within 3 days.

Butternut Squash Soup Base

Squash is a versatile vegetable and can be prepared in a number of ways from soups to pasta and as dessert. Squash can be an excellent base for a creamy soup and is probably my wife's favorite. This soup base can be reserved for winter days when you need a tasty, warm soup. It is made with only a few ingredients so that leaves plenty of room for you to be creative when you add it to your soups. Recipe makes 7 quarts.

Ingredients:

- 3 cups of chicken stock
- 4 lbs. of butternut squash
- 2 cups of water, or as needed
- Salt and ground black pepper, to taste

Directions:

1. Set up your All American® pressure canner and sterilize jars and lids. Leave them in steady simmering water until needed.
2. Peel squash and cut long wise. Take out seeds and slice into 1 inch pieces lengthwise then into cubes. Put water and squash into a large pot and boil for 2 minutes.
3. Remove squash from water with a slotted spoon, try not to mash cubes. Put squash into jars along with stock, season with salt and pepper and leave 1 inch of headspace. Make sure there are no air bubbles and wipe the rims of the jars and lids. Close jars as tightly as possible and place them into the prepared pressure cooker. Process the squash with a pressure of 10 pounds for 90 minutes. If you are using pint size jars, pressure for 55 minutes.

Chicken Corn Chowder Base

This is the corn and chicken base for making the chowder. Do not add the cream to this mixture as it will not preserve well and could be unsafe for storage. Dairy should never be added to bases especially when they contain meat. Recipe makes 5 pints.

Ingredients:

4 chicken thighs, deboned and skinned

1 cup onion, minced

3 cups potatoes, cubed

4 cups chicken broth

1 tsp. of salt

1/3 cup celery, diced

2 cups of Corn

Directions:

1. Cube vegetables and chicken.
2. Put broth into a large pot and heat until simmering. Remove from flame.
3. Put prepared jars on a clean dish towel. Start layering ingredients into jar starting with chicken, potatoes and then vegetables. Then put the broth into jars, leave 1 inch of headspace. Make sure there are no air bubbles. Wipe the rims and lids of the jars with vinegar.
4. Close jars as tightly as possible. Close lid of pressure canner and bring to a boil then allow steam to vent for 10 minutes. Close vent and pressure at 10 lbs for 75 minutes. If you are using quart sized jars pressure for 90 minutes.

5. Turn off heat when soup has finished pressuring and let gauge return to zero. Remove lid from pressure canner and let jars sit for 10 minutes inside before removing. Place jars on a clean towel and let them sit overnight undisturbed.
6. If jars make a popping sound that means they are cooling and sealing. Check seals and redo any unsealed jar. Store until needed.
7. To make soup creamy before serving, add ¼ cup milk or cream and 1 tsp. cilantro or thyme. Heat over a medium flame until soup is thoroughly heated. Add pepper and salt to taste.

Clam Chowder Soup Base

This clam chowder base can be used to prepare your next bowl of creamy clam soup. Clams can become rubbery so add your cream to this mixture whenever you are ready to serve. Saves half the time and it can be stored up to 6 months.

Ingredients:

- 1 cup onions, chopped
- 8 cups of potatoes, peeled and chopped
- ½ lb bacon, diced
- 12 cups clams with juice
- 8 cups of boiling water
- Black pepper and salt to taste

Directions:

1. Heat a large saucepan and lightly brown the bacon. Place bacon on paper towels to drain excess fat. Add onion to bacon grease and cook until tender; do not brown. Add in potatoes, water and clams and juice. Add salt and pepper to the mixture.
2. Put prepared jars on a clean dish towel. Fill jars using a ladle, being sure to leave 1 inch of headspace. Make sure there are no air bubbles. Wipe the rims and lids of the jars with vinegar.
3. Close jars as tightly as possible. Close pressure canner lid and bring to a boil then allow steam to vent for 10 minutes. Close vent and pressure at 10 lbs for 100 minutes.
4. Let gauge return to zero. Remove lid from the pressure canner and let jars sit for 10 minutes before removing. Place jars on a clean towel and let them sit overnight undisturbed. Add cream, to taste, before serving.

Vegetable Broth

This is a basic broth that can be used as a base for many soups or as added flavor for other dishes. When you are making this broth do not can the actual vegetables in it. The flavors of the vegetables are infused into the broth from cooking. Add more vegetables to achieve a more complex flavor. I really like the following combo but every time I make this, it's different as I often use what I have on hand.

Ingredients:

- 1 onion, chopped
- 2 carrots, chopped
- 8 garlic cloves, diced
- 6 sprigs thyme
- 1 tsp. of salt
- 1 tbsp. olive oil
- 2 celery with leaves, chopped
- 1 cup scallions, chopped
- 8 sprigs of parsley
- 2 bay leaves
- 2 quarts of water

Directions:

1. Heat oil in a large pot and sauté vegetables. Cook for 5 minutes stirring constantly. Pour in water and salt and simmer for 30 minutes. Strain broth and discard vegetables.

2. Put prepared jars on a clean dish towel. Fill jars with broth using a ladle; be sure to leave 1inch headspace. Make sure there are no air bubbles. Wipe the rims and lids of the jars with vinegar.

3. Add jars to the pressure canner and close the lid. Bring to a boil and allow steam to vent for 10 minutes. Close vent and pressure at 10 lbs for 75 minutes or pressure for 90 minutes if using quart jars.
4. Once the pressure canner has been depressurized and vented, remove jars from the canner and put them on a towel on the counter to cool. Let the jars sit for at least 12 hours without being disturbed. Then, check all seals. Store safely sealed jars for up to 1 year in a cool, dark place.

SMOOTH AND EASY FENNEL AND CARROT SOUP

This is a highly nourishing soup made with aromatic fennel and sweet carrots. Serve this soup as a first course at dinner or with a grilled sandwich for lunch. It is a good soup to have on hand during the cold and flu season. Both the fennel and the carrots have valuable antioxidants, as well as high concentrations of vitamins and minerals able to help the body fight off illness. This recipe makes 6 quarts of soup.

INGREDIENTS:

- 2 bulbs of fennel, thinly sliced
- 2 tbsp. olive oil
- 4 lbs. carrots, peeled and sliced
- 6 cups vegetable stock
- 6 cups water
- 1/2 tsp. white pepper
- pickling salt, to taste

DIRECTIONS:

1. Heat olive oil over medium heat in a heavy stainless steel pot. Add sliced fennel and sauté until fennel is clear and soft. Add carrots and vegetable stock, then bring to a boil. Turn heat down to low and let simmer. When carrots are tender remove from heat.

2. Use a blender to puree the soup. Put the puree back in the pot over medium heat. Stir in the water, season with pepper and salt, and simmer for another 30 minutes, stirring occasionally.

3. While the soup is simmering, set up your All American® pressure canner. Sterilize jars and lids. Keep them in hot water until they are needed.

4. Pour the hot soup into the hot jars, making sure to leave a headspace of 1 inch. Use a damp paper towel to wipe jar rims and threads. Put the lids on and tighten rings.

5. Carefully put the jars in the All American® and process at 10 pounds of pressure for 35 minutes. After following depressurizing and venting steps, take the jars out of the canner. Put them on a towel on the counter to cool completely, undisturbed.

16 Bean Soup

Beans are full of nutrients and should be a staple of every diet. They are high in protein and fiber and virtually fat free. When beans are cooked they usually don't last very long which is why this is such a great recipe to can. This soup is quite filling and hearty and great to consume on those winter days. Lots of veggies along with the ham make it very flavorful. When you are ready for some rich bean soup just pull out a jar, heat and enjoy. Recipe Makes 6 pints.

Ingredients:

- 4 onions
- 4 garlic cloves, minced
- 6 carrots
- 16 oz. canned tomatoes, diced
- 1 ham bone
- 3 tsp. pepper
- 32 oz. beans soup pack
- 1 ½ celery stalk, chopped
- 2 bay leaves
- 16 oz. canned green chilies, diced
- 4 cups ham, chopped
- 3 tsp. Kosher salt
- 14 cups of water

Directions:

1. Set up your All American® canner, sterilize jars (8-10 pints) and lids, and keep them in simmering water until ready to use.

2. Sort and wash beans, then put them into a large pot along with 6 cups of water and bring to a boil. Boil 2 minutes, remove from heat and soak for 2 hours.

3. Add the remaining ingredients to beans and cook for 1 ¾ hours. Do not boil soup, but heat it until it is hot and just barely simmering. Remove ham bone from soup and spoon into jars leaving 1inch headspace. Wipe the rims of the jars and lids. Close jars as tightly as possible and pressure at 10 lbs for 1 hour. Pressure jars for 75 minutes if you are using quart jars.

4. Canned soup will be very thick due to expansion of beans. Add stock to soup before serving.

BEANS AND SALSA SOUP

Black beans are high in soluble fiber and can help lower our cholesterol. Use your favorite store bought or homemade salsa for this recipe. This soup could easily be made into a dip by mashing beans and reducing some of the liquid. Have this soup as is or thicken it and pair with rice or your favorite bread. Recipe makes 7 pints.

INGREDIENTS:

- 2 cups of dried black beans
- 1 Onion, chopped
- 1 tbsp. Cumin
- 1 pint Salsa
- 6 cups chicken broth

DIRECTIONS:

1. Set up the All American®, sterilize jars and lids, and keep them in simmering water until ready to use.
2. Sort and wash beans then put into a large pot along with 6 cups broth and bring to a boil. Remove from heat and soak for 1 hour. Beans will be half cooked but will finish cooking when pressured.
3. Using pint size jars put beans, onions, salsa and a dash of cumin in each. Fill each jar about half way with mixture then put in hot broth leaving 1inch headspace. Make sure there are no air bubbles.
4. Wipe the rims of the jars and lids with a clean cloth. Close jars as tightly as possible and place into pressure canner. Close lid and bring to a boil then allow steam to vent for 10 minutes. Close vent and pressure at 10 lbs for 75 minutes. If you are using quart sized jars pressure for 90 minutes.
5. Turn off heat when beans have finished pressuring and let gauge return to zero. Remove lid from pressure canner and let jars sit for 10 minutes

inside before removing. Place jars on a clean towel and let them sit overnight undisturbed.

CHICKEN GARBANZO SOUP

I got into Garbanzo beans initially because of some health benefits I read about but I keep coming back to them because they are so good. Like other legumes, they can help in insulin regulation. Garbanzo beans are both healthy and delicious. They are paired with chicken in this soup to create a satisfying blend. Recipe makes 6-8 pints.

INGREDIENTS:

1 lb. garbanzo beans or chickpeas

4 cups of chicken broth

1 tsp. salt

3 lbs. chicken breast, skinned and deboned

1 cup diced onions

1 medium Jalapeno pepper

1 tsp. crushed black pepper

DIRECTIONS:

1. Put garbanzos into a large pot along with enough water to cover them, apply medium-high heat and bring to a boil. Remove pot from heat and let it stand for 1 hour. Add more water and simmer for 30 minutes. Do not bring the water to a boil to avoid splitting the peas.
2. Put prepared jars on a clean dish towel and put ½ cup beans on the bottom of the jars. Divide jalapeños and onions equally and add it into the jars. Season each jar with a pinch of ground pepper and salt. Add in the chicken and pour in the broth leaving 1 inch of headspace. Make sure there are no air bubbles.

3. Wipe the rims of the jars clean and close jars as tightly as possible. Close lid to pressure canner and bring to a boil then allow steam to vent for 10 minutes. Close vent and pressure at 10 pounds for 75 minutes. If you are using quart sized jars pressure for 90 minutes.

4. Turn off heat when beans have finished pressuring and let gauge return to zero. Remove lid from pressure canner and let jars sit for 10 minutes inside before removing. Place jars on a clean towel and let them sit overnight undisturbed.

LAYERED CHICKEN SOUP

Chicken soup is a delight to have on a pantry shelf when the days are cool and the nights cold. It is especially welcome during the cold and flu season. This layered chicken soup is as attractive as it is delicious, making it a great choice for a get well gift. It's a nice way to let the older members of your community know that you're thinking about them. Alternate light and dark colors or go from lightest to darkest when layering this soup into your canning jars. Use blanched fresh vegetables or frozen vegetables that have been thawed. This recipe makes two quarts, but can easily be doubled.

INGREDIENTS:

2 cups peeled, diced potatoes

2 cups carrots, sliced

1 1/3 cups corn

1 1/3 cups green beans

2/3 cup peas

1 cup cooked chicken meat

2 tbsp. onion, chopped

¼ cup chopped fresh Roma tomatoes

2 quarts chicken broth

Directions:

1. Prepare canning equipment. Set up your All American®, sterilize jars and lids, and keep them in simmering water until ready to use.
2. Bring the chicken broth to a boil in a medium saucepan. While waiting for the broth to boil, pack the sterile, hot jars, arranging the ingredients attractively and leaving a full inch of head-space.
3. Pour the hot broth over the soup ingredients, filling the jars up to the 1-inch head-space. Wipe the threads and rims of the jars, then top with a lid. Tighten rings, then put in the pressure canner. Process at 10 pounds of pressure for 90 minutes.
4. After the All American® depressurizes and is ready to open, remove the jars and let cool undisturbed. Check jar seals at 24 hours. Store sealed jars in a cool, dark place for up to 12 months.

ITALIAN MEATBALL SOUP

This soup gives you a creative way to use meatballs and it's great for when you want some comfort food. Put your favorite blends into your meatballs and make this soup just the way you like. I love canning meat and being able to pull something like this out of the pantry anytime I like. This is one of those recipes that I am not able to let sit for too long as I always seem to be in the mood for meatballs! Recipe makes 6-8 pints.

INGREDIENTS:

- 1 cup diced onions
- 1 medium stalk of celery, chopped
- 5 cups chicken stock
- 20 frozen meats balls, thawed
- 3 ½ cups canned white beans, drained
- ½ tsp salt, or more to taste
- ½ tbsp. olive oil
- 4 garlic cloves, minced
- 4 medium carrots, diced
- 2 to 2 ½ cups of water, for sterilizing jars
- 1 cup loosely packed baby spinach, coarsely chopped
- ½ tsp. black pepper, coarsely ground

DIRECTIONS:

1. Put oil into frying pan and apply medium-high heat. Once the oil is hot, sauté the garlic, carrots, onions and celery for about 4 minutes or until lightly browned. Season to taste with salt and pepper. Cook ingredients for 1 minute while stirring regularly. Remove from pan and set aside.

2. Pour the broth into a pot over medium-high heat and cook for 5 minutes. Remove pot from heat and keep covered.

3. Put prepared jars on a clean dish towel and put ½ cup beans on the bottom of jars. Divide and add the spinach, vegetables, onions and stir in 3 meatballs. Pour the stock into each jar using a funnel and leave 1inch headspace. Make sure there are no air bubbles and wipe the rims and lids of the jars well.

4. Close jars as tightly as possible and close pressure canner lid, bring to a boil and allow to steam for 10 minutes with open steam vent. Close the vent and pressure at 10 pounds for 75 minutes. If you are using quart sized jars pressure for 90 minutes.

5. Turn off heat when the beans have finished pressuring and the let gauge return to zero. Remove lid from pressure canner and let jars sit for 10 minutes inside the canner before removing. Place jars on a clean towel and let them sit overnight undisturbed.

FRENCH ONION SOUP

This base is perfect for whenever you are in the mood for some scrumptious onion soup. Just grab a can, add your cheese and whatever else you desire to your soup and enjoy! This onion soup is made with beef broth and red wine. Simple ingredients blend together to great a truly rich taste.

INGREDIENTS:

- 1 tsp. olive oil
- ½ cup red wine
- 1 tsp. dried thyme
- 8 cups onions, sliced into rings
- 1 ½ cups of water
- 8 cups beef stock
- ½ tbsp. ground black pepper

DIRECTIONS:

1. Put oil into frying pan and heat. Cook onions in batches for about 15 minutes each. Do not overgrown the onions. The pressure canner will finish the cooking process. Remove from pan and put aside till needed. Pour broth, wine, pepper, water and thyme into a pot and heat for 5 minutes. Remove from heat and keep covered.

2. Put prepared jars on a clean dish towel and put ½ cup onions in the bottom of jars. Add in broth into jars using a funnel, leave 1inch headspace. Make sure there are no air bubbles. Wipe the rims and lids of the jars.

3. Close jars as tightly as possible. Close lid and bring to a boil then allow steam to vent for 10 minutes. Close vent and pressure at 10 pounds for 60 minutes. If you are using quart sized jars pressure for 75 minutes.

4. Turn off heat when the onions have finished pressuring and let gauge return to zero. Remove lid from pressure canner, and let the jars sit for 10 minutes inside to cool before removing them.

POTATO AND LEEK SOUP

Leeks are a part of the onion and garlic family and have a mild onion taste. This is a traditional, flavorful soup that can be made whenever leeks are in season. The potatoes will remain firm and over time marinate with all the flavors of the broth and leeks. This soup can be eaten hot or cold. Who doesn't love potato soup?

INGREDIENTS:

- 5 lbs. leeks, cleaned and sliced into rounds
- 6 potatoes
- 6 cups beef stock

DIRECTIONS:

1. Soak leeks to clean them and slice into rings; put aside till needed. Peel potatoes and put in cold water till needed. Put prepared jars on a clean dish towel and layer leeks in the bottom of jars. Then put in potatoes and top with more leeks. Add broth to jars using a funnel, leave 1inch headspace. Make sure there are no air bubbles. Wipe the rims and lids of the jars.
2. Close jars as tightly as possible. Close pressure canner lid and bring to a boil and allow steam to vent for 10 minutes. Close vent and pressure at 10 pounds for 60 minutes. If you are using quart sized jars pressure for 75 minutes.

3. Turn off heat when soup has finished pressuring and let gauge return to zero. Remove the lid of the pressure canner and let the jars sit for 10 minutes inside to cool before removing.

"Hoowee!" Chili

Ground beef or venison can be used to make this hearty and spicy chili. A pint of chili can serve 2-3. When preparing, add as little or as much of the ingredients as you please. This Mexican delight can be enjoyed by everyone and can be served with rice or other staples. Do not make your chili too thick when canning so that it can be processed thoroughly. Recipe makes 9 pints.

Ingredients:

- 3 lbs. ground venison or beef
- 3 cups cooked beans
- 2 bell peppers, seeds removed and chopped
- 2 cayenne peppers, diced
- 1 tsp. salt
- 1 tsp. garlic powder
- 2 dozen Roma tomatoes, seeds removed and chopped
- 2 onions, chopped
- 2 Jalapeño pepper, diced
- 2 tsp. cumin
- 2 tsp. chili powder
- 1 tbsp. Cocoa powder

Directions:

1. Heat a skillet, add a little oil and put in onion and meat and cook until browned. Put in beans, tomatoes, seasoning and peppers and cook until vegetables are soft. Add water if necessary, sauce should not be too thick.

2. While the chili cooks, set up the pressure canner and sterilize the jars and lids. Keep them submerged in simmering water until you are ready to use them.

3. Spoon the chili into prepared jars leaving 1inch headspace. Wipe the rims of the jars and lids with a cloth. Close jars as tightly as possible and pressure at 15 lbs for 75 minutes.

4. Once the pressure canner has been depressurized and vented, remove jars from the canner and put them on a towel on the counter to cool. Let the jars sit for at least 12 hours without being disturbed. Then, check all seals. Store safely sealed jars for up to 1 year in a cool, dark place.

MUSHROOM CAP SOUP

I thought about calling this one, Mix and Match Mushroom Maniac soup but that would be getting carried away. (Dial it back in, Skip!) Use whatever mushrooms you can get your hands on for this one. No matter what type of mushroom you prefer all mushroom have many beneficial nutrients. They are an antioxidant, full of vitamin D and help to boost your immune system amongst many other benefits. This soup may be seasoned and had as is or you may add cream for the traditional cream of mushroom soup. Recipe makes 5 pints.

INGREDIENTS:

2 ½ mushrooms, remove stalks

1 ½ tsp. thyme

6 garlic cloves

8 cups of vegetable broth

¼ tsp. Nutmeg, if so desired

DIRECTIONS:

1. Slice the mushrooms and mince the garlic. Set aside until needed.
2. Heat broth in a large pot. Add thyme and nutmeg. When heated, remove from heat, but keep covered.
3. Put prepared jars on a clean dish towel. Fill jars with mushrooms about ¾ ways full and add 1 tsp. garlic. Then put broth into jars, leaving 1inch headspace. Make sure there are no air bubbles. Wipe the rims and lids of the jars with vinegar.
4. Close jars as tightly as possible. Close pressure canner lid and bring to a boil then allow steam to vent for 10 minutes. Close vent and pressure at 10 lbs for 75 minutes. If you are using quart sized jars pressure for 90 minutes.

5. Turn off heat when mushrooms have finished pressuring and let gauge return to zero. Remove lid from pressure canner and let jars sit for 10 minutes inside before removing. Place jars on a clean towel and let them sit overnight undisturbed.
6. To make soup creamy add 1/8 cup flour and tbsp. butter. Whisk together then add some liquid from jar and whisk until smooth. Add in the rest of the mushroom soup. Put in cream to taste and stir to combine till soup is thick.

TOMATO AND ROASTED RED PEPPER SOUP

Tomato soup is loved and consumed worldwide. The added red pepper adds dimension and flavor to an already great concoction. The roasted ingredients in this soup definitely give it a bold taste. If you're like me, you'll have to grill a cheese sandwich for dipping. Recipe makes 5 quarts.

INGREDIENTS:

15 lbs. red Peppers, seeds removed

8 garlic cloves

1 tsp. beef bouillon

20 lbs. tomatoes, seeds removed and pureed

1 ½ Sweet onion, sliced

½ cup sugar

1 tsp. smoked paprika

6 cups of water

DIRECTIONS:

1. Set oven to 500°F. Slice peppers into quarters and discard seeds and membranes. Place peppers, garlic and onion onto a greased baking sheet and bake until skin of peppers turn black. Remove from heat and cover with foil. Remove skin of peppers when cooled.

2. Put roasted vegetables and remaining ingredients into a large pot along with water. Simmer for an hour, avoid boiling mixture. Let the mixture cook until reduced by half. Use an immersion blender to puree and cook for an additional 5 minutes. Remove from flame. Add soup into the jars using a funnel, leaving 1 inch of headspace. Make sure there are no air bubbles. Wipe the rims and lids of the jars with vinegar. Close jars as tightly as possible. Close lid and bring to a boil then allow steam to vent for 10 minutes. Close vent and pressure

at 10 lbs for 85 minutes. If you are using pint sized jars pressure for 65 minutes.

3. Turn off heat when soup has finished pressuring and let gauge return to zero. Remove lid from pressure canner and let jars sit for 10 minutes inside before removing.

4. I recommend adding a dash of cream to the soup before serving.

Condensed Tomato Soup (using Clear Jel)

Tomato soup is usually made with a flour roux however it is unsafe to can flour as it spoils easily. We have replaced it with a specialized thickening agent (Clear Jel). It leaves no taste to the soup base. Just grab a jar of this soup base, add your milk or broth, heat and enjoy! Recipe makes 4 pints.

Ingredients:

- 8 lbs. tomatoes, chopped
- 2 cups of onion, minced
- 1 cup of fresh parsley
- ¾ cup clear jel
- 1 cup celery, chopped
- 1 red pepper, seeds removed and minced
- 6 bay leaves
- 2 ½ tbsp. salt
- 1-2 tbsp. oil
- 4 tbsp. lemon juice

Directions:

1. Heat a large pot and add a little oil. Put in celery, pepper, tomatoes and onion; stir to combine and bring to a boil. (The juice from the tomatoes will be enough to build a small boil. Add bay leaves and parsley and cook until vegetables are tender. Stir frequently.
2. Remove from flame, cool then press through a food mill into another large pot. Reserve ½ cup of the puree and mix with clear jel. Heat soup in the pot then add clear jel mixture and boil for 2 minutes until soup thickens.

3. Spoon tomato soup into prepared pint jars. Add a tbsp. of lemon juice being sure to leave 1 inch of headspace. Wipe the rims of the jars and lids with a clean cloth.
4. Close jars as tightly as possible and pressure at 10 lbs for 25 minutes. Avoid using quarts for this recipe but you may use ½ pint jars.
5. When canner has depressurized, remove jars and allow to cool for at least 12 hours.
6. When ready to use your canned soup, just mix with equal parts of another liquid. I recommend chicken broth or milk, with a splash of cream.

German Beef Stew

The combination of apple cider vinegar and red wine vinegar makes this stew a real taste sensation – ideal for home preserving, and the perfect backdrop to all those nourishing vegetables and meat. I never consider my pantry complete without at least a few jars of this stew ready to go. Heat the stew before serving, and season with more peppers and gingersnaps if desired. Dish up over rice or egg noodles, and enjoy this hearty winter classic!

Ingredients:

- 5 lbs. beef bottom round
- 2 cups of water
- 1 cup of apple cider vinegar
- 1 cup of red wine vinegar
- 2 medium-sized white onions, chopped
- 2 large carrots, peeled and chopped
- Pinch of salt and pepper
- 4 bay leaves
- 10 whole cloves
- 20 juniper berries
- 2 tsp. of mustard seeds
- 2/3 cup of white sugar

Directions:

1. Sterilize your canning jars and lids in a bath of hot – but not boiling – water.
2. In a large stovetop saucepan, heat the cider vinegar, wine vinegar, water, salt, pepper, bay leaves, cloves, juniper, mustard seeds and

sugar. Cover the saucepan and bring the ingredients to a boil, then reduce the heat and simmer for 10 minutes.

3. Cut the beef into bite-sized chunks no wider than 1 inch, and set aside.
4. Place the hot jars on a dishtowel, and fill each with equal portions of chopped onions and carrots, then add equal portions of the raw cubed beef on top.
5. Remove the bay leaves from the hot simmering ingredients, and use a funnel to pour the hot liquid into the jars, leaving a 1-inch headspace at the top.
6. Remove the air bubbles from each jar using a plastic spatula, and refill with more liquid to the 1-inch mark as needed. Moisten a clean paper towel with vinegar and wipe around the rims of each of the jars. Add the lids and sealing rings to the tops of each jar and seal them finger-tight.
7. Place jars in your All American® and close the lid. Bring to a boil then allow steam to vent for 10 minutes. Close vent and pressure at 10 lbs for 90 minutes for quart jars and 75 minutes for pint jars.
8. When processing time is up, turn off the heat but leave the canner on the stove with the lid on, until the pressure returns to zero on its own. A few minutes after the pressure has returned to zero, open the vent and remove the canner lid.
9. Wait 10 minutes, then remove the jars from the canner using tongs, and set them on a dishtowel to cool overnight. Do not touch or move them for at least 12 hours. When jars are cooled, check to make sure they sealed properly and store in a cool, dark place.

Chili Con Carne

Canning your favorite convenience foods at home is a great way to clean up your diet. Read the ingredient lists on a few different brands of factory-canned chili and compare those ingredients to those used in this recipe. Canning your own chili means no artificial flavors, colors and other assorted food additives. Instead, you have a pantry shelf full of convenient, heat and eat chili made with ingredients you can trust. This recipe makes 9 pints.

Ingredients:

Beans

- 3 cups dried pinto or kidney beans
- 5 ½ cups water
- 2 tsp. salt

Meat

- 3 lbs. ground venison or lean ground beef
- 1 ½ cups chopped onion
- 1 cup sweet or hot peppers, chopped (optional)
- 1 tbsp. salt
- 1 tsp. black pepper
- 3 to 6 tbsp. chili powder
- 8 cups crushed or whole tomatoes

Directions:

1. Pick over and wash beans thoroughly, then put them in a heavy stainless steel pot and add enough cold water to cover beans by at

least 2 inches. Put a lid on the pot and leave the beans to soak for 12 to 18 hours.

2. When the beans have soaked long enough, pour them into a colander to drain away the soaking liquid. Return the beans to the pot and pour in 5 ½ cups water. Stir in 2 tsp. of salt. Bring the pot to boiling over medium-high heat. Decrease the temperature to medium-low, let the beans simmer for 30 minutes, then drain them.

3. While the beans simmer, prepare your All American® for processing. Sterilize 9 pint jars and lids. Keep them sterile by leaving them in hot, almost simmering water until the jars and lids are needed.

4. In the same pot used to cook the beans, over medium heat, brown venison or ground beef with the onions and peppers. Pour off fat. Return the drained beans to the pot. Stir in the remaining ingredients, then simmer everything together for another 5 minutes.

5. Ladle the hot chile con carne into hot jars, leaving 1 inch of headspace. Wipe jar rims and threads clean with a damp paper towel. Top each jar with a hot lid and tighten rings. Carefully put the jars into the pressure canner and process at 10 pounds of pressure for 75 minutes.

6. Once the pressure canner has been depressurized and vented, remove jars from canner and put them on a towel on the counter to cool. Let the jars sit for at least 12 hours without being disturbed. Then, check all seals. Store safely sealed jars for up to 1 year in a cool, dark place.

7. If a jar has not sealed as it should have, store it in the refrigerator and use the chili within 3 days.

2
MEATS & MAIN DISHES

SAUSAGE AND PEPPERS

Homemade sausages would be best for this recipe but store bought can substitute. Sausage must be precooked before canning to eliminate as much fat as possible. Your favorite type of hot pepper could also be added but be careful not to overdo it. Remember, the sausages will be infused with the flavors it is canned with as time goes on. Recipe makes 5 quarts.

INGREDIENTS:

- 20 sausage links
- 2 yellow onions
- 3 bell peppers
- 4 quarts of beef broth

DIRECTIONS:

1. Slice onions and cut pepper into strips. If you are using pint size jars, cut sausages in half. Heat a frying pan, use a paper towel with a bit of oil and grease pot. Sauté onions and peppers for 10 minutes till they are browned lightly. Remove from heat and put aside. Using the same pan cook sausage and drain on paper towels to remove excess fat. Heat stock, remove from heat but keep hot.

2. Put prepared jars on a clean dish towel. Fill jars with sausage, onion, pepper mixture then add in broth; being sure to leave 1inch headspace. Make sure there are no air bubbles. Wipe the rims and lids of the jars with vinegar.

3. Close jars as tightly as possible. Close pressure canner lid and bring to a boil then allow steam to vent for 10 minutes. Close vent and pressure at 10 lbs for 90 minutes. Let gauge return to zero. Remove lid from pressure canner and let jars sit for 10 minutes inside before removing. Place jars on a clean towel and let them sit overnight undisturbed.

SANDRA MAY

Corned Beef Hash

I'm a sucker for this one. It's a perfect breakfast, lunch, dinner...or snack? Seriously, eat it whenever. You can cook it with or without onions. It's filling and satisfying and apparently a big deal on St. Patrick's Day (among other things). Recipe makes 7 pints.

Ingredients:

- 5 large potatoes, peeled
- Hot water, as needed
- 1 tsp. of crushed black pepper
- ½ lb of corned beef, rinsed and cubed
- 1 white onion, diced (optional)
- ½ tsp. of salt

Directions:

1. Cut the potatoes into half lengthwise and thinly slice, trim corned beef and cut into cubes. Add them in a large bowl and mix to combine. You may add onions in the mixture if desired. Season with salt and ground pepper. Scoop the hash into prepared pint jars and add boiling water to cover the ingredients, plus 1 inch. Wipe the rims and lids of the sterilized jars with dry cloth.

2. Close the jars tightly and place them into the prepared pressure canner. Close the lid and apply medium heat, bring to a boil and steam for 10 minutes with open steam vent. Close vent and pressure at 10 pounds for 75 minutes. If you are using quart sized jars pressure for 90 minutes. When finished allow jars to remain in pressure canner for 10 minutes to begin to cool. Remove jars and place them on a towel to cool overnight.

3. Drain water from hash before serving and cook with or without extra onions.

Chicken and Vegetable All-Purpose Head-Start

This recipe offers an all purpose head-start on a busy day's evening meal. Open a jar and you have the basic ingredients for a casserole, pasta dish, rice dish, or soup, prepared and ready to heat and use. This practical addition to your pantry shelves is sure to be appreciated again and again when time is tight and everybody's hungry. While this is made with chicken, you can also substitute rabbit or squirrel for the chicken.

Makes: 7 - 8 pints.

Ingredients:

8 to 10 lbs. chicken, rabbit or squirrel cut in pieces

1 tbsp. salt

½ tsp. pepper

1 tbsp. chopped fresh parsley

Water to cover

1 cup chopped onion

2 cups chopped celery

2 cups thin sliced peeled carrots

Directions:

1. Put the meat in a heavy pot with the salt and pepper. Add water to cover and bring to boiling over high heat. Reduce heat to medium-low and simmer until meat is ready to fall from bones. Remove from heat. Let cool until meat can be handled.

2. While meat is cooling, prepare your All American®. Set up the pressure canner, sterilize jars and lids. Keep the jars and lids in simmering water until ready to use them.

3. Pull the meat from the bones and set aside. Keep broth, discard bones, skin and fat. Be thorough in removing fat, so it doesn't move up the jar sides during the processing and cooling phases to prevent jars from sealing correctly.

4. Add the vegetables to broth and bring to boiling, then stir in the meat pieces. Use a slotted spoon to take the hot meat and vegetables from the broth to fill the jars, leaving 1 inch of head-space. Pour the boiling liquid into the jars, stopping at the 1-inch head-space.

5. Wipe threads and rims of jars, then put on lids and tighten rings. Arrange jars in the pressure canner and process at 10 pounds for 75 minutes, adjusting for altitude as needed. When safe to open canner, remove jars without tilting and leave to cool undisturbed. Check all seals after 24 hours, then store in a cool, dark place for up to one year.

Almost Done Beef Stroganoff

This delightful Beef Stroganoff is exactly the sort of thing you want to keep your pantry shelves stocked with. It is a delicious, almost done main dish in a jar. All it needs is a couple quick finishing touches. When the Beef Stroganoff first comes out of the jar, it will have to boiled for 10 minutes in an uncovered pan. You'll need to make some rice or pasta to serve it over and add a bit of sour cream and cornstarch while heating. This recipe makes 5 pints and each pint serves two.

Ingredients:

- 3 lbs. of round steak, cut in cubes
- ½ cup of butter
- 1 ½ cups diced white onion
- 2 tsp. of minced garlic
- 4 cups halved fresh mushrooms
- ½ cup sherry wine, optional
- 3 to 4 tbsp. of tomato paste
- 2 cups of beef stock, or as needed to fill the jars

Directions:

1. Heat the oven to 450 degrees Fahrenheit. Put the beef cubes in a baking pan and put the beef in the oven to brown. After 10 minutes, turn the cubes and brown them for another 10 minutes.
2. Melt the butter in a pot over medium heat. Add onions and garlic sautéing them until soft and tender. Stir in the mushrooms and sauté for another 3 minutes. Pour in the wine and simmer until it has fully evaporated. Add the tomato paste and the stock, cook until it reaches a boil.
3. Prepare the pressure canner for processing. Sterilize 5 pint jars and lids with steady simmering water until needed.

4. Divide the meat and add into the hot jars. Pour in the dripping sauce from the baking pan into the stock. Use a slotted spoon to transfer the mushroom mixture into the jars. Pour the stock into the jars, preserving the 1-inch of headspace. If the prepared stock is not enough, heat some water or extra beef stock to add into the jar. Use a chopstick or thin plastic spatula to break up any air bubbles or air pockets.

5. Wipe the rim and threads of each jar with a damp paper towel or damp lint-free cloth. Put on the hot lids and tighten the rings. Place the jars into the All American® pressure canner and process the jars at 10 pounds of pressure for 75 minutes.

6. Let the canner depressurize itself, a process that will take at least 30 minutes. Prepare a spot on the counter for the jars. Spread a towel out to protect the counter-top. Transfer the jars from the canner to the towel to cool.

7. Do not move the jars for at least 12 hours, then you can check the seals. Jars with a good seal can be stored in a cool, dark spot for up to 12 months. If there is a jar that did not seal properly, store it in the refrigerator and use the Beef Stroganoff within 3 days.

8. Before serving the Beef Stroganoff, empty the jar into a saucepan and boil it for 10 full minutes, uncovered.

9. Stir together ¼ cup sour cream and 1 tbsp. of cornstarch for each pint jar you are serving. Stir the sour cream-cornstarch mixture into the Beef Stroganoff while heating it right before serving, not during the 10 minute boil right after it comes out of the jar. Serve over hot buttered egg noodles or rice.

Spaghetti Sauce with Ground Venison

This is a simple and elegant spaghetti sauce, using time-honored, traditional ingredients, like fresh tomatoes, garlic, onion, bell pepper and basil. The ground venison is a special touch, adding a bit more depth to the flavor of the sauce. If venison isn't available, you can use very lean ground beef in its place. Serve this sauce over cheese ravioli or pasta for a quick meal after a long day. Tomato sauces are endlessly useful and versatile, used to prepare all kinds of food. This is a pantry shelf item that is every bit as practical as it is delicious. This recipe makes 6 to 7 pints.

Ingredients:

- 5 lbs. ground venison
- 6 quarts tomatoes, peeled and chopped
- 1 onion, chopped
- 2 cups chopped bell pepper
- ¼ cup chopped parsley
- 2 cloves garlic, minced
- 1 ½ tbsp. salt
- 1 tbsp. sugar
- 1 tbsp. sweet basil, crumbled

Directions:

1. In a large stainless steel pot, cook onion and venison together over medium heat until the venison is no longer pink. Pour off the fat. Add the rest of the ingredients to the pot and, stirring frequently, simmer for 1 hour or until sauce has thickened enough.
2. While the sauce simmers, set up the pressure canner. Sterilize the jars and lids, then leave them in the simmering water until needed.

3. When the sauce is thick enough, bring it to a full boil, then remove from heat. Pour the hot spaghetti sauce into the hot jars, leaving a full inch of headspace. Carefully wipe the threads and rim of each jar with a damp paper towel. Close with hot tops and tighten the rings securely.

4. Put the jars in the pressure canner and process pint jars at 10 pounds of pressure for 75 minutes or for 90 minutes if using quart jars. After completing the depressurization and venting steps, remove the jars from the canner and set on a towel to cool.

5. Check seals after jars have sat undisturbed for at least 12 hours. Jars that sealed nicely can be stored for up to 12 months in a cool, dark place. If you see a jar that didn't seal correctly, store it in the refrigerator and use the tomato sauce within three days.

CHICKEN, CORN AND LENTIL SPRING MIX

This combo of chicken, corn and lentils is an absolute crowd pleaser. It's simple to make, tasty and healthy. You'll come back to it again and again. Recipe makes 5 quarts (10 pints)

INGREDIENTS:

3 cups of dried lentils

2 tsp. of salt

5 lbs. of boneless, skinless white-meat chicken

1 tbsp. of olive oil for sautéing the chicken

2 cups of sweetcorn, either fresh or frozen and thawed

1 cup of fresh spring onion, rinsed and diced

3 tsp. of ground paprika

6 cups of chicken broth

DIRECTIONS:

1. Prepare the lentils by removing any debris and rinsing in cool water. Leave them to soak in a large pot for 12-18 hours.
2. When ready to can, prepare your canner and sterilize jars. Leave the jars in hot water until ready to use.
3. Drain lentils and add 6 cups of fresh water and 2 tsp salt. Bring to a boil, then reduce heat and simmer for 30 minutes. Drain when cook time is complete.
4. Trim the chicken of any fat and cut into small cubes (approximately 1 inch). Use a frying pan to sauté the chicken in a small bit of olive oil. Make sure chicken is cooked through, but not overdone. Add the onions and stir several times to distribute the oil and allow for equal sautéing. After onions have softened, place chicken and onions on a plate and dab off excess oil with a paper towel.
5. In a large pot, heat chicken broth to a simmer. Add the paprika and corn, continuing to simmer for a few more minutes until all ingredients are hot and well incorporated.
6. Portion the chicken and onions equally into the prepared jars. Add the lentils. Use a ladle or funnel to pour the hot chicken broth mixture into the jars, making sure to leave an inch of headspace. Remove any air bubbles and wipe the jars clean. Apply lids and tighten rings until they are finger tight.
7. Place the jars carefully into the prepared All American® and secure the lid. Heat to a boiling and allow the steam to vent for 10 minutes before closing and securing the steam vent. Process at 10 pounds of pressure setting the timer for 90 minutes. (75 minutes for pint jars.)
8. After the pressure has returned to zero, remove the lid and allow jars to sit for a few more minutes. Remove from the canner and place in a safe spot to allow to cool completely before checking to be sure that all jars have sealed properly.

Asian Turkey Meatballs

This one is always a hit around my house. These meatballs have a sweet, but spicy taste. You just can't go wrong with homemade meatballs. Have I mentioned my love of meatballs? I always have to leave some out to fill up on as I can the rest. Be sure not to overcook your turkey as it dries out quickly. Recipe makes 10 pints.

Ingredients:

- 5 medium stalks of scallions, chopped
- 5 garlic cloves, minced
- 1 tsp. of black pepper
- 3 tbsp. of light soy sauce
- 3 lbs. ground turkey
- 1-inch piece of fresh ginger root, grated
- 1 tbsp. of salt
- 3 tbsp. of Teriyaki sauce
- ½ tbsp. of garlic powder
- 6 cups of low-sodium chicken broth or stock
- ½ to 1 tsp. of crushed red pepper flakes, or as needed for extra heat
- Oil, for greasing

Directions:

1. Set oven to 350°F. Put all ingredients, except chicken stock and oil for greasing the pan, into a mixing bowl and combine thoroughly with hands. Roll mixture into balls and place them on a greased baking sheet. Bake for 45 minutes or until the meatballs are brown and remove from oven. Cover baking sheet with foil to keep it warm.

2. Place the chicken stock in a pot and apply medium heat until it starts to form bubbles. Do not bring to a boil. Put prepared jars on a clean dish towel and add in the hot meatballs. Ladle in the warm stock just enough to cover the meatballs by 1 inch and leaving 1 inch of headspace. Make sure there are no air bubbles. Wipe the rims and lids of the jars with vinegar.

3. Close jars as tightly as possible and place them into the prepared pressure canner. Close lid, apply heat and bring to a boil. Let it steam for 10 minutes with open steam vent. Close the vent and pressure at 10 pounds for 75 minutes or pressure for 90 minutes if using quart jars.

4. When canner has reached zero pressure, cool jars for approximately 10 minutes before removing from the canner. Place jars on a towel in a safe space to cool completely. Check seals after at least 12 hours. Jars that have sealed properly can be stored in a cool, dark place for 12 months. Jars that did not seal properly should be placed in the refrigerator and used within 3-5 days.

Chicken Meatballs

These meatballs are infused with a Southwestern taste. But you can flavor your chicken meatballs as you like. Just be sure to follow correct processing procedures and you will have a tasty batch to last for a long time. These meatballs have a similar taste to tamales. Recipe makes 10 pints.

Ingredients:

- 4 lbs. of ground chicken meat
- 3 tbsp. of garlic powder
- 2 tbsp. smoky salt
- 2 tbsp. of poultry seasoning
- 1 cup of freeze-dried shallots
- 1 tsp. of crushed black pepper
- ½ tsp. of crushed red pepper flakes
- 2 tbsp. of ground cumin
- 3 tbsp. of paprika
- 5 cups of chicken stock

Directions:

1. Put all ingredients, except for chicken stock, into a mixing bowl and combine thoroughly with hands. Cover bowl and put in refrigerator overnight to allow the flavors to infuse. Set oven to 350°F. Divide and roll the mixture into small balls or use a scoop and place on a greased baking sheet. Bake for 30-40 minutes or until brown and remove from oven. Cover baking sheet with foil to keep it warm.
2. Place the stock in a pot and apply medium heat until it starts to form bubbles. Do not bring it to a boil. Put the prepared jars on a clean dish

towel and add the hot meatballs. Pour in the warm stock to cover the meatballs by 1 inch and leave 1 inch of headspace.

3. Make sure there are no air bubbles. Wipe the rims and lids of the jars with vinegar. Close the jars tightly and place them into the prepared pressure canner. Close lid and apply heat. Bring to a boil and then let it steam for 10 minutes with open steam vent. Close vent and pressure at 10 pounds for 75 minutes or pressure for 90 minutes if using quart jars.

4. Once the pressure canner has been depressurized and vented, remove jars and set them on a towel to cool. Let them sit, undisturbed, for at least 12 hours, then check seals. Put correctly sealed jars in a cool, dark place for up to 12 months.

BEEF BOURGUIGNON

Beef Bourguignon not only sounds impressive (It's French!), but it's delicious and by canning it you can have an easy and exciting meal with very little effort. If you have guests coming over…bust out the bourguignon. Be sure to say it with a flourish. Your friends will think you're a crazy goofball, but they'll put up with that and more when they taste this dish!

INGREDIENTS:

- 5 lbs. of beef steak
- 2 medium-sized white onions, peeled and chopped
- 1 cup of brown or white button mushrooms, rinsed and sliced
- 1 cup of pearl onions, peeled and diced
- 5 cloves of garlic, peeled and minced
- 1 tbsp. of dried ground thyme
- 1 tbsp. of dried ground bay leaf
- 1 tbsp. of dried ground sage
- 3 cups of red Burgundy wine
- 3 cups of beef broth

DIRECTIONS:

1. Begin by trimming the fat from your steaks and placing them in a large stockpot on the stovetop. Add the pearl onions and pour in the beef broth and red wine. Bring the liquid to a boil, then reduce the heat and simmer for about 15 minutes.
2. Remove the steak from the broth and carefully cut it into 2 inch cubes. The steak should still be rare on the inside.
3. Add the steak cubes back into the broth and add the remaining ingredients. Continue to simmer for about 25 more minutes.

4. While the broth is simmering, prepare your All American® canner and jars. Keep the jars in hot water, that is not quite boiling, until ready to use.

5. Fill each jar with equal portions of the steak and vegetables. Use a ladle or funnel to pour the broth into each jar being sure to reserve one inch of headspace. Remove any air bubbles with a plastic knife or spatula. Use a damp cloth to clean the jars and threads. Add the lids and tighten the rings until finger tight.

6. Place the jars into the All American® and close the lids. Bring canner to a boil and allow steam to vent for 10 minutes. After 10 minutes, close the vent and process at 10 pounds of pressure for 90 minutes if using quart jars and 75 minutes if using pint jars.

7. When jars are done processing, turn off the heat source. When the pressure has returned to zero, remove the lid. After several minutes remove the jars from the canner and place them on a towel covered counter to cool.

8. Allow jars to cool for at least 12 hours before checking to make sure they have sealed properly. If jars make a popping noise while they are cooling, it is just them sealing correctly. Store correctly sealed jars in a cool, dark place for up to one year. Place any unsealed jars in the refrigerator and use within a few days.

Chicken Pot Pie Filling

Making chicken pot pie can be easy if you already have the prepared filling started. This recipe uses raw meat so be sure to be careful to sanitize all equipment properly. When ready to use use your filling, use whatever you like to use as a thickener (flour, cornstarch) and I like to add a bit of cream. Then just pour into a prepared pie crust and cook according to the direction of your crust. Recipe makes 7 pints.

Ingredients:

- 1 tbsp. of oil
- 2 cups diced carrots
- 1 large white onion, diced
- 2 ½ lbs. of cooked chicken breasts, deboned and cubed
- 1 tsp. of salt
- ½ tsp. of crushed black pepper
- 6 cups of chicken stock
- 1 cup of diced celery stalk
- 1 cup canned peas
- Hot water or stock, as needed to fill the jars
- 1 tbsp. of mixed Italian dried herbs

Directions:

1. Remove excess fat from chicken, rinse and pat dry with paper towel. Season the chicken with crushed pepper and salt. Heat a skillet with medium-high heat and add the oil. Lightly brown the chicken on all sides and remove from heat. Place on a plate and cover with foil to keep it warm.

2. Put prepared jars on a clean dish towel. Fill the jars with evenly divided browned chicken, vegetables and herbs. Pour the chicken stock into a pot and heat over medium heat until it just begins to bubble, but do not boil. Remove from the stove and pour the stock into the jars to cover 1 inch above the ingredients, leaving 1 inch of headspace. Make sure there are no air bubbles and wipe the rims and lids of the jars with vinegar.

3. Close jars as tightly as possible and place them into the prepared pressure canner. Close lid and apply heat. Bring to a boil and allow steam for 10 minutes with open steam vent. Close the vent and pressure at 10 pounds for 75 minutes or pressure for 90 minutes if using quart jars.

4. When canner gas cooled, remove jars and place on a towel in a quiet place to allow them to cool overnight. Store properly sealed jars in a cool, dark place and use within a year.

SWEET AND SOUR CHICKEN

Sweet and sour chicken is usually fried and then covered in sauce. This canned version is much healthier and without a doubt just as delicious as the traditional dish. You'll thank me for this one. Recipe makes 5 quarts.

INGREDIENTS:

- 2 medium green bell peppers, seeded and diced
- 2 cups of diced white onions
- ½ to ¾ cup of raw cane sugar
- 5 to 6 tbsp. of light soy sauce
- ½ tbsp. of ground ginger
- 4 ½ lbs. of cooked chicken breast, deboned and cubed
- 1 large red bell pepper, diced
- 6 cups of canned pineapple chunks
- 1 cup of cane or white vinegar
- ¼ cup of tomato ketchup
- ½ cup of water
- ½ cup fresh pineapple juice

DIRECTIONS:

1. In a pan over medium-high heat, add the sugar, soy sauce, ginger, vinegar, ketchup, ½ of cup water and pineapple juice and cook until the sugar is fully dissolved while stirring regularly. Remove from heat.
2. Put prepared jars on a clean dish towel. Fill jars with cubed chicken, diced peppers, onions and pineapple chunks. Pour in the warm liquid mixture just enough to cover 1 inch above the ingredients. Make sure

there are no air bubbles. Wipe the rims and lids of the jars with vinegar.

3. Close the jars as tightly as possible and place them into the prepared pressure canner. Close lid and bring to a boil. Let it steam for 10 minutes with open steam vent. Close the vent and pressure at 10 pounds for 90 minutes. If you are using pint sized jars pressure for 75 minutes.

4. Let gauge return to zero. Remove lid from pressure canner and let jars sit for 10 minutes inside before removing. Place jars on a clean towel and let them sit until cool, at least 12 hours.

Mushroom, Spinach and Chicken Medley

Having lots of healthy and tasty canned food in my pantry makes it really easy to avoid junk food. I don't have any excuses especially when what I have on hand is so good. This is a good one if you need something to do with a lot of fresh spinach. Recipe makes 5 quarts (10 pints)

Ingredients:

- 5 lbs. of boneless, skinless white-meat chicken
- 12 pounds of fresh harvested spinach
- 2 cups of white or brown mutton mushrooms, rinsed and sliced
- 1 tbsp. of olive oil (for sautéing the mushrooms)
- 5 cloves of garlic, peeled and minced
- 1 ½ cups of white wine (any kind will do, fine to use the cheap stuff)
- 5 cups of chicken broth

Directions:

1. Prepare your jars for canning and keep them in hot, but not boiling water until ready to be filled.
2. Clean and prepare the spinach. Use your hands or a knife to tear the spinach into large pieces. Steam the spinach until it is just wilted then set aside for later use.
3. Use the stovetop to bring the chicken broth to a boil. Add the wine and simmer the liquids for 15 minutes.
4. Use a sauté pan to briefly sauté the mushrooms and garlic in a bit of olive oil until they are just softening and fragrant. Drain the grease by placing them on a paper towel. Use the same sauté pan and oil to brown the chicken on all sides. Use a dry paper towel to blot off the grease when the chicken is done.

5. Divide the spinach equally amongst the prepared jars. Add mushrooms and garlic and top with the chicken. Ladle the hot broth and wine mixture into the jars. Use a plastic knife to remove any air bubbles and be sure to reserve 1 inch of headspace. Wipe clean any debris or liquid that may prevent jars from sealing and close the lids until finger tight.

6. Place jars inside the prepared All American® and secure the lid. When steam begin to escape the vent, set the timer for 10 minutes. After 10 minutes, close the vent and set the pressure to 10 pounds. Process quart jars for 90 minutes and pint jars for 75 minutes. When time is up remove the source of heat, but leave the lid for several more minutes.

7. After a few minutes, remove the lid and allow jars to sit undisturbed for about 10 minutes. At this time carefully remove the jars and place somewhere that they can cool, undisturbed overnight. Check seals and store properly sealed jars in a good, dark storage space. Any jars that did not seal properly should be placed in the fridge and used within a few days.

Chicken Cacciatore

This Italian delight is delicious over a hot serving of rice or pasta and can come in handy for those days you need something filling but don't want to cook. Though this recipe uses chicken thighs, the bones are removed as boneless meat is easier and safer to process. Recipe makes 5 pints.

Ingredients:

- 9 chicken thighs, skin and bones removed
- 3 garlic cloves, diced
- 1 onion, halved and sliced
- 2 pints canned tomatoes, diced
- ¾ lbs. mushrooms, chopped
- ¼ cup dried oregano
- 2 cups chicken broth
- 1-2 tbsp. oil

Directions:

1. Heat skillet or frying pan, add a little oil then add chicken and cook until golden all over (no need to cook thoroughly, pressuring will cook the chicken the rest of the way).
2. Remove chicken from pot and set aside. Drizzle a bit more oil in the pan and add mushroom, garlic, tomatoes, onions, broth and oregano. Cook for 15 minutes, stirring frequently; remove from flame.
3. Add 2-3 pieces of chicken to each prepared jar. Then add tomato mixture leaving 1 inch of headspace. Wipe the rims of the jars and lids with a clean cloth dampened with vinegar. Close jars as tightly as possible and pressure at 10 lbs for 75 minutes or 90 minutes if using quarts.

4. When canner has depressurized, allow jars to remain for a few more minutes, before removing. Place cans in a safe place to allow to sit overnight. If jars make a popping sound that means they are cooling and sealing. Check seals and store jars in a cool, dark space until needed.

PULLED PORK

I'm a southerner, which means everyone I know loves pulled pork. For this recipe just flavor your pork anyway you prefer as long as it is cooked soft enough to be shredded. Be sure to take the proper precautions when canning meats so as to avoid it being unsafe for storage.

INGREDIENTS:

- 4 to 5 lbs. of barbecued pork meat, shredded
- 2 cups of beef brown stock
- 1 tsp. of ground black pepper
- ¼ cup of barbecue sauce
- 1 tbsp. of homemade or ready made dry rub
- Vinegar, for brushing the lid and rim of jars

DIRECTIONS:

1. Season the pork meat with dry rub, ground pepper and barbecue sauce and toss to evenly coat the meat. Reheat it before canning and heat the stock in a pot. Do not bring to a boil.

2. Put prepared jars on a clean dish towel. Fill jars with pork ¾ ways then add in broth; be sure to leave 1 inch of headspace. Make sure there are no air bubbles. Wipe the rims and lids of the jars with vinegar.

3. Close jars as tightly as possible and place them into the prepared pressure canner. Close the lid and bring to a boil. Let it steam for 10 minutes with open steam vent. Close the steam vent and process with a pressure of 10 pounds for 75 minutes. If you are using quart sized jars pressure for 90 minutes.

4. When canner has reached zero pressure, cool jars for approximately 10 minutes before removing from the canner. Place jars on a towel in

a safe space to cool completely. Check seals after at least 12 hours. Jars that have sealed properly can be stored in a cool, dark place for 12 months. Jars that did not seal properly should be placed in the refrigerator and used within 3-5 days.

APPLE BUTTER PORK

You can choose to make your own apple butter for this dish. This recipe will come in handy and is quite soft and delectable. When preparing meats for canning, be sure to eliminate as much fat from the meat as possible. The meat will keep for a longer time if there are not a lot of fats.

INGREDIENTS:

- 3 to 4 cups of pork loin, trimmed and silver skin removed, sliced into strips or cubed
- ¼ cup of apple butter
- 2 to 3 tbsp. of stock
- ¼ tsp. of clove spice powder
- 2 cups of apple juice
- 3 to 4 tbsp. of raw cane sugar
- ½ tsp. of cinnamon spice powder
- 1 tsp. of salt
- ½ tsp. of crushed black pepper

Directions:

1. Set oven to 350°F. Remove excess fat and silver skin from the pork loin and cut into strips or cubes. Season meat with salt and crushed black pepper and place it in a greased baking dish. Bake for an hour or until brown and remove from the oven.
2. While baking the meat, add the sugar, cloves, cinnamon, apple butter and stock in a pot over medium-high heat. Bring to a boil while stirring regularly. Remove from heat, spread the mixture on the baked meat and toss to evenly coat the meat with the apple butter sauce. Return the meat into the oven and bake for another 1 hour.
3. Heat apple juice in a pan over medium heat until it starts to simmer. Remove from heat and do not bring to a boil.
4. Put prepared jars on a clean dish towel. Fill the jars with pork, pour in the apple juice just enough to cover the meat. Be sure to leave 1 inch of headspace in the jar. Make sure there are no air bubbles and wipe the rims and lids of the jars with vinegar.
5. Close the jars tightly and place them into the prepared pressure canner. Close the lid and bring to a boil. Let it steam for 10 minutes with open steam vent. Close the steam vent and process with a pressure of 10 pounds for 90 minutes.
6. When canner has reached zero pressure, cool jars for approximately 10 minutes before removing from the canner. Place jars on a towel in a safe space to cool completely. Check seals after at least 12 hours. Jars that have sealed properly can be stored in a cool, dark place for 12 months. Jars that did not seal properly should be placed in the refrigerator and used within 3-5 days.

RASCALLY RABBIT

Rabbit is a versatile meat that can be compared to chicken. Rabbits can be reared and eaten young or old; both stages provide a variety in taste. Canning time differs based on if meat is boneless or not; it is best to leave the bone in when canning rabbit. Recipe makes 6 pints.

INGREDIENTS:

6 lbs. of rabbit meat, bone-in or lean meat

2 cups of beef stock

½ cup red wine

1 tbsp. of mixed Italian herbs

Salt and crushed black pepper, to taste

DIRECTIONS:

1. Cut rabbit meat into large cubes that can fit inside the jar. Heat the stock in a pot over medium-high heat, and add the red wine, mixed dried herbs, salt and pepper. Place rabbit into the pot and bring to a boil. Cook until meat is no longer pink. Remove from heat and transfer to a plate.
2. Pack rabbit into the prepared jars and pour in the cooking stock leaving 1inch headspace. Wipe the rims of the jars and lids and close jars as tightly as possible. Place the jars into the prepared pressure canner, close the lid and process with a pressure 10 pounds for 1 hour. Pressure jars for 75 minutes if you are using quart jars.
3. Once the pressure canner has been depressurized and vented, remove jars from the canner and put them on a towel on the counter to cool. Let the jars sit for at least 12 hours without being disturbed. Then, check all seals. Store safely sealed jars for up to 1 year in a cool, dark place.

Turkey Sausage

Turkey meat is both fun to cook and to eat. It being a bit leaner than beef makes me feel better about eating it for some reason. I've come to love the taste and having sausage in the pantry ready to go is such a plus. You beef lovers can certainly use beef instead with this recipe. You'll love the flavor. Recipe makes 10 pints (5 quarts)

Ingredients:

- 6 lbs. of lean ground turkey meat
- 2 medium-sized onions, grated
- 1 ½ tbsp. of dried sage
- 1 tbsp. of dried rosemary
- 6 large cloves of garlic, peeled and finely minced
- 5 tsp. of salt
- 2 tsp. of ground black pepper
- 5 cups of heated chicken broth

Directions:

1. Prepare your All American® and sterilize your jars, leaving them in hot, but not boiling, water until ready for use.
2. Use a large mixing bowl to thoroughly mix together the ground turkey, onions and all the seasonings. Form the turkey mixture into sausages about the size of a large finger.
3. Lightly grease a baking tray and line up the sausages on the tray. Bake for 45 minutes in a preheated oven at 350 degrees.
4. When the sausages are close to being done in the oven, bring the chicken broth to a simmer on the stovetop.

5. Place the cooked turkey sausages into the prepared jars, filling the jars about ¾ full. Use a funnel to pour the hot broth into the jars on top of the sausage being sure to leave 1 inch of headspace.

6. Remove any air bubbles and clean up the jars from any liquid or debris that would prevent jars from sealing properly. Top with lids and apply sealing rings.

7. Place jars carefully into the canner and make sure lid is secure. Once the steam begins to escape the vent, set a timer for 10 minutes. After 10 minutes, seal the steam vent and set the gauge for 10 pounds of pressure. Process for 75 minutes for pint jars (90 minutes for quart jars).

8. When gauge has returned to zero, wait for about 10 minutes before removing the jars. Being careful not to jostle or shake them, place the jars on a towel covered counter where they can cool, undisturbed for at least 12 hours.

9. Check to make sure that jars have been properly sealed. Place properly sealed jars in a cool, dark storage space for up to one year. If a jar did not seal properly it will need to be refrigerated and used within 3 days.

Chicken

Canned chicken is super handy to have around to prepare a last minute soup or casserole. I've even seasoned some up to prepare chicken nachos for a late night snack! You may can chicken with either bone in or out according to your preference. If you leave the skin on, just know that it may be a bit mushy. Can your own chickens or watch the sales at the store and be prepared when the craving for chicken nachos strikes! Yields about 2 quarts, depending on the size of chicken and if you leave the bone in or remove it.

Ingredients:

5-6 lbs. of chicken of your choice

1 tsp. salt

Directions:

1. Separate chicken at the joint or remove completely from bone. Remove skin if desired. Pack chicken loosely into prepared jars. Add 1/2 tsp salt to each jar. Be sure to leave 1 inch of headspace.

2. Remove any air bubbles and use a vinegar wipe to clean the threads to the jars. You may hot pack with boiling water or broth if you like, or use the raw pack method with no liquid as chicken will produce its own. If you add liquid, remember to leave an inch of headspace.

3. Apply lids and rings securely. Place in your prepared All American® canner. Process at 10 lbs of pressure. Boneless chicken should process for 1 hour and 30 minutes. Chicken with bones still in should process for 1 hour and 15 minutes.

4. When processing is complete, remove jars and place them on a counter covered with a towel. Allow to cool, undisturbed before checking seals.

Lemon Salmon in Vinaigrette

I'm a big, big fan of canning fish. Make a large batch and you can enjoy it year round. This is an elegant combination of flavor using common ingredients you probably already have around your kitchen. Recipe makes 5 quarts (10 pints)

Ingredients:

- 6 lbs. of fresh wild salmon
- 5 quarts of brine (one cup of salt to one gallon of water)
- 3 medium-sized lemons
- 2 tbsp. of olive oil
- 3 cups of balsamic vinegar

Directions:

1. Remove any fat you see on the fish and cut the fish into strips about 1 ½ inches thick. Prepare the brine and add the salmon. Soak for at least one hour before draining and discarding the brine.
2. Prepare the canner, jars and lids. Jars and lids should remain in hot, but not boiling water until just before use.
3. Cut the lemons into slices and set aside. In a deep bowl, add the olive oil and vinegar, whisking quickly until the two are well blended into a vinaigrette.
4. Place prepared jars on the counter and divide the lemon equally, placing in the bottoms of the jars. Pack with the salmon. Skins should face outward, touching the glass, packing jars tightly, but not overfilling. Ideally, they will be about ¾ full.
5. Using a funnel to top the salmon with the prepared vinaigrette. Reserve one inch of headspace. Remove any air bubbles with a plastic knife or spatula. Carefully wipe a moist paper towel over the jars and threads before applying lids and sealing rings.

6. With jars placed carefully in the All American®, secure the lid. When water reaches a boil, allow steam to vent for 10 minutes before closing the steam vent. Set the pressure gauge for 10 pounds of pressure and process quart jars for 200 minutes (140 minutes for pint jars.)
7. When timer is up and gauge has returned to zero, carefully remove the lid. Let jars sit for another few minutes before removing to a towel covered counter. Jars will need to cool for at least 12 hours before checking to make sure the jars were sealed properly.
8. This salmon is best served cold, as a perfect topping for a salad or a snack right out of the jar.

GARLIC LEMON TROUT

Ready to get sophisticated? This dish rivals anything you'll find on a restaurant menu. It's the perfect combination of the garlic and lemon flavors to go with a tender fish like Trout. Serving: Drain away the excess lemon juice, and serve the canned trout cold or warm, either over a fresh salad, or as the topper to a pasta or rice of your choice. Enjoy!

Recipe makes 5 quarts (10 pints)

INGREDIENTS:

6 lbs. of fresh trout

5 quarts of brine (one cup of salt to one gallon of water)

50 medium-sized lemons

25 medium-sized cloves of garlic, peeled and crushed

DIRECTIONS:

1. Prepare the fish into strips that are about 1-1 ½ inches but no bigger. Make sure to have removed as much of the fat as possible. Add the fish to the brine and soak for at least one hour.

2. While the trout is in the brine, squeeze the lemons. Add lemon juice to the crushed garlic.

3. Remove trout from the brine and place equal portions into prepared quart or pint jars. The skins should face outward, touching the glass. Pack jars tightly, about 3/4 filled. Ladle in the lemon juice-garlic mixture and fill to the one inch mark. Remove any air bubbles with a plastic knife or spatula and refill as needed to maintain one inch of headspace.

4. Use a damp cloth to wipe the jars and threads clean before applying the lids and rings.

5. Place jars into the prepared canner and secure the lid. Allow steam to vent for 10 minutes before closing the steam vent. Process the jars at 10 pounds of pressure for 200 minutes for quart jars or 140 minutes for pint jars.

6. When timer sounds, allow jars to sit in the canner for about 10 more minutes before removing. Carefully place the jars on a counter or table to cool for at least 12 hours without being moved or touched.

Tuna

Tuna is widely consumed in many dishes, but you can't be sure of the process that canned tuna goes through. Canning your own tuna provides a way for you to have your tuna in whatever spices you please. Try not to slice your tuna fish too thick so that it can't be thoroughly processed. If you cannot access freshly caught tuna, you may use frozen. Recipe makes 4 pints.

Ingredients:

- 2 lbs. tuna
- 4 tsp. Kosher salt
- 8 tsp. extra virgin olive oil
- 2 tsp. black pepper

Directions:

1. Slice tuna into ½ inch pieces crossways. Add 2 tsp. of oil to each jar.
2. Pack tuna into jars by layering, first place tuna with cut side down into jar and top with pepper and salt; repeat until jar is full. You may use other spices if desired. Be sure to leave 1inch headspace, if any spaces are left fill with pieces of tuna. Use a plastic knife or otherwise to remove air bubbles. Wipe the rims of the jars and lids.
3. Close jars as tightly as possible and pressure at 10 lbs for 100 minutes.
4. Let gauge return to zero. Remove lid from pressure canner and let jars sit for 10 minutes inside before removing. Place jars on a clean towel and let them sit overnight undisturbed.
5. If jars make a popping sound that means they are cooling and sealing. Check seals, any jars not sealed can be refrigerated and eaten within 7 days.
6. Canned tuna can be stored for up to a year on a cool dark place.

Salmon

Fish takes the longest time to process when it comes to pressure canning. When canning fish be sure to soak fish in salt water. Remove bones from larger fish and leave bones in smaller fish. Make sure you store fish in pint size jars as larger jars may not be able to get rid of bacteria when canning fish.

Ingredients:

3 lbs. salmon

Salt

Directions:

1. It's best to go with freshly caught salmon if you can. Keep fish chilled until you are ready to put it in the pressure canner. Dissolve 1 cup of salt in a gallon of water. Cut fish into pieces that can fit in the pint jars.
2. Soak fish for an hour in the salt water and then drain. Put prepared jars on a clean dish towel. Fill jars with salmon with skin side against glass. Fish can be packed in the jars tightly, but be sure to leave 1 inch of headspace. Wipe the rims and lids of the jars with vinegar.
3. Close lid and bring to a boil then allow steam to vent for 10 minutes. Close vent and pressure at 10 lbs for 100 minutes.
4. When canner has depressurized, allow jars to cool for 10 minutes before removing them from the pressure canner. Place the jars on a towel on the counter and leave them undisturbed for 12 hours. Store in a cool, dark place.

SANDRA MAY

GARLIC MUSHROOM CHICKEN IN TOMATO SAUCE

I've enjoyed this recipe often. It's a simple yet saucy, rich meal. And it's healthy! You can't go wrong with these flavor combinations. Recipe makes 5 quarts (10 pints)

INGREDIENTS:

- 6 lbs. of boneless, skinless chicken
- 2 pints of tomato sauce
- 2 tbsp. of extra-virgin olive oil for stovetop sautéing
- 3 cups of white or brown mutton mushrooms, rinsed and sliced
- 1 medium-sized white onion, peeled and diced
- 1 tbsp. of dried oregano
- 1 tbsp. of dried basil
- ½ cup of heated chicken broth
- 3 cloves of fresh garlic, peeled and minced

DIRECTIONS:

1. Trim as much fat as you can from the chicken then cut into strips that are no more than 1 1/2 inches thick. Use a frying pan to sauté the chicken in olive oil until all sides are brown. Drain all excess oil and pat dry with a paper towel.
2. Add the remaining ingredients to a large stockpot and simmer lightly over medium low heat for approximately 10 minutes.
3. Prepare you canner and sterilize the jars. Keep the jars in hot water until ready for use.
4. Place jars on a counter and divide the chicken equally amongst the jars. Use a funnel to pour in the hot tomato mixture, being sure to

reserve 1 inch of headspace. Take the time to remove any air bubbles and refill jars if needed.

5. Use a cloth moisten with vinegar to wipe the jars and threads clean before applying the lids and rings.

6. With the jars safely inside the canner, close the lid and turn on the heat. Allow steam to vent for ten minutes. Close the vent and pressure at 10 pounds of pressure for 90 minutes. (75 minutes for pint jars)

7. When processing is complete, allow jars to cool for 10 minutes before removing to a towel covered counter. Leave the jars to cool for at least 12 hours. Check seals and store properly for later enjoyment.

SLOPPY JOES

These are an American original. This mix will be quick and easy. Remember to use as little fat as possible when preparing meats for canning.

INGREDIENTS:

2 lbs. ground beef

1 tsp. vegetable oil

3 tsp. Worcestershire sauce

¼ cup water

2 tbsp. apple cider vinegar

1 cup onion

1 ½ cups ketchup

2 tbsp. brown sugar

2 tsp. mustard

DIRECTIONS:

1. Prepare canning equipment. Set up the pressure canner, sterilize pint jars and lids, and keep them in simmering water until ready to use
2. Put oil in a large pot, heat and cook onion and beef until beef is browned and onion is soft and translucent. Remove from pan and drain carefully, being sure to remove as much of the fat as possible. Transfer to a large cooking pot. Put in all remaining ingredients, stir and simmer for 20 minutes. Remove from heat.
3. Put prepared jars on a clean dish towel. Fill jars with sloppy joe using a ladle; being sure to leave 1 inch of headspace. Make sure there are no air bubbles. Wipe the rims and lids of the jars with vinegar.
4. Add jars to your pressure canner, close the lid and bring to a boil. Allow steam to vent for 10 minutes. Close vent and pressure pints at 10 lbs for 75 minutes or pressure quarts for 90 minutes.
5. Let gauge return to zero. Remove lid from pressure canner and let jars sit for 10 minutes inside before removing. Place jars on a clean towel and let them sit overnight to cool.

TACO MEAT

Tacos are definitely a lifesaver when you need a quick meal to feed a crowd. This recipe is very versatile as you can add any flavor salsa or add different vegetables to suit your own taste. The taco seasoning can be made in advanced and used as needed. Add ¼ cup of seasoning per 2 lbs of meat. Recipe makes about 18 pints.

INGREDIENTS:

- 16 oz black beans
- 8 cups corn
- 4 cups water
- 4 cups beef broth
- 8 lbs. Ground beef
- 8 cups salsa

Taco seasoning: (use 1 cup in recipe, store the rest in your cupboard to have on hand)

- 4 tbsp. paprika
- 3 tbsp. Mexican oregano
- 3 tbsp. ground cumin
- 10 tbsp. chili powder (can be more or less)
- 4 tbsp. onion powder
- 1 tbsp. sea salt
- 4 tbsp. sugar
- 2 tbsp. garlic powder
- 8 tbsp. clear jel
- 4 tbsp. cocoa powder

2 tbsp. citric acid

DIRECTIONS:

1. Place beans in a container and cover them with water. Leave overnight to soak. Put all ingredients for taco seasoning into a blender and pulse to combine; store in a quart jar until needed.
2. Prepare canning equipment. Set up the pressure canner, sterilize jars and lids, and keep them in simmering water until ready to use.
3. Drain water from beans and place into a large pot with 4 cups of water.
4. Cook over a low flame for 30 minutes; avoid boiling the beans as they may split.
5. Heat skillet and cook beef until browned, remove from skillet and place on paper towels to remove excess oil. You may also use a colander to rinse the meat with warm, running water. This will remove much of the fat.
6. Add beef to beans along with all other ingredients, including 1 cup of the taco seasoning. Cook for 10 minutes. Mixture will not be thick.
7. Spoon taco mixture into jars leaving 1inch headspace. Wipe the rims of the jars and lids with a clean cloth dampened with vinegar. Close jars as tightly as possible and pressure at 10 lbs for 75 minutes and at 10 lbs for 90 minutes if using quarts.
8. Let gauge return to zero. Remove lid from pressure canner and let jars sit for 10 minutes inside before removing. Place jars on a clean towel and let them sit overnight undisturbed.

3

Bean Recipes

Summer BBQ Beans

Peruano beans are much creamier than pinto beans and are great in this molasses blend. Pair these beans with your favorite grilled meats and send your taste buds on a journey. Add some freshly chopped jalapeno or chili peppers to make this blend spicy. I am firmly on team molasses and can eat it with most anything. It doesn't take much to add a punch of flavor, but add more according to taste. I think that 3 tbsp. is a good amount for this recipe. Recipe makes 5-6 quarts.

Ingredients:

- 4 cups of water (plus more for soaking/cooking beans)
- 1 tbsp. white vinegar
- ¾ tsp. dry mustard
- 1 red onion, chopped
- 2 lbs. Peruano beans
- 3 tbsp. dark molasses
- 2 tsp. Kosher salt
- 1 cup brown sugar

Directions:

1. In a Dutch oven or a large pot, heat approximately 8 cups of water and the beans. Bring to a boil and remove from heat. Cover pot and put aside for beans to soak for 45 minutes. Drain beans and add onion and an additional 8 cups of water. Cook beans for 15 minutes. Put water (4 cups), vinegar, mustard, molasses, sugar and salt in a sauce pan; stir to combine. Bring mixture to a boil. Taste and make adjustments as needed. Sauce will be thin, but flavorful.

2. Use a slotted spoon to put beans and onions into jars about ¾ ways full. Then spoon in sauce, leaving 1 inch of headspace. Wipe the rims

of the jars and lids. Close jars as tightly as possible and pressure at 10 lbs for 75 minutes. If you are using pint size jars, pressure for 55 minutes.

3. Once the pressure canner has been depressurized and vented, remove jars from the canner and put them on a towel on the counter to cool. Let the jars sit for at least 12 hours without being disturbed. Then, check all seals. Store safely sealed jars for up to 1 year in a cool, dark place.

Back Home Pork and Beans

Commercially canned pork and beans are typically navy beans in a mild, tomato-based sauce with a barely-there scrap of pork fat, just enough to let its makers legally label it pork and beans. That tiny scrap of legal technicality that is present in each factory-produced can of pork and beans provides a clear example of why there has been such a surge of interest in home food production, including gardening and home canning. This recipe brings canned pork and beans back home, where it belongs. The next can of pork and beans you open can be made of flavorful, nourishing real food, far better for you than legal technicalities, labeling loopholes and food additives. This recipe makes 3 quart jars or 6 pint jars.

Ingredients:

- 1 quart dried navy beans
- ¼ lb salt pork
- 1 quart tomato juice
- 3 tbsp. sugar
- 2 tsp. salt
- 1 cup chopped onion
- ¼ tsp. cloves
- ¼ tsp. allspice

Directions:

1. Pick through dry beans, removing any bad beans, pebbles, twigs or other debris. Wash beans in a colander under cold running water.
2. Put the navy beans in a large, heavy stainless steel pot. Pour in enough cold water to cover the beans, put the lid on the pot and put the beans in a cool place for 12 to 18 hours.

3. After soaking, drain the beans and return to the pot. Pour boiling water over the beans, then bring the pot to boiling over high heat. Lower the heat to medium-high and boil for 3 minutes. Take the pot off of the heat and let it sit for 10 minutes. Drain the beans again.

4. While the beans sit, set up the pressure canner and sterilize the jars and lids. Keep them submerged in simmering water until you are ready to use them.

5. Put 1 cup of hot beans into each hot jar, then follow with a piece of salt pork. Fill each jar up to the ¾ mark with beans.

6. Bring tomato juice, sugar, salt, onion and spices to a boil in the large pot. Pour the boiling liquid over the beans to fill the jars, leaving 1 inch of headspace.

7. Wipe the rim and threads of each jar, then add the lids. Tighten the rings and put the jars into the pressure canner to process. Pints need to process for 65 minutes under 10 pounds of pressure. Process quarts for 75 minutes, also at 10 pounds of pressure.

8. After the processing time is completed, let gauge return to zero. Remove lid from the pressure canner and let jars sit for 10 minutes before removing. Place jars on a clean towel and let them sit overnight undisturbed.

Ranch Style Beans

These beans are effortless to make but have a big burst of flavor. Make these in advance for the summer season. Pair these beans with grilled meat for a true 'ranch' taste. They can be stored for up to a year. Recipe makes 5 pints.

Ingredients:

- 2 cups of pinto beans
- 6 garlic cloves, minced
- 2 cups of canned diced tomatoes
- 1 tbsp. of apple cider vinegar
- ½ tbsp. ground cumin
- 4 to 5 cups of beef brown stock
- 3 to 4 tbsp. ground chili powder
- 1 large white onion, diced
- 1 tbsp. oil
- ½ tbsp. of raw cane sugar
- ½ tbsp. of smoked paprika
- 1 tsp. of dried oregano leaves
- ½ tsp. of salt
- ½ tsp. of crushed black pepper

Directions:

1. Sort beans and soak overnight in a container with water. After soaking the beans, drain and transfer into a pot. Pour in enough water to cover the beans, apply medium-high heat and cook for 30 minutes. Remove pot from heat and drain the beans just before using.

2. Heat the oil in a sauté pan over medium-high heat and sauté the onions for 10 minutes. Stir in the garlic and sauté for another minute. Remove from heat and let it rest to cool.

3. Transfer the garlic and onion into a blender together with the sugar, paprika, oregano, chili powder, tomatoes, vinegar, cumin and 1 cup of water. Puree the ingredients until it is smooth and season with salt and black pepper. Transfer to a large bowl and mix in the beans. Set aside.

4. Heat the stock in a pot over medium-high heat until it starts to form bubbles. Do not bring to a boil. Remove the pot from heat, but do not remove the lid to keep it warm.

5. Put prepared jars on a clean dish towel. Fill the jars with bean and puree mixture about ¾ full. Pour in the stock and leave 1inch headspace. Make sure there are no air bubbles and wipe the rims and lids of the jars with a dry cloth.

6. Cover the jars tightly and place them in the prepared pressure canner. Close canner lid and bring to a boil. Let it steam for 10 minutes with open steam vent. Close the vent and process with a pressure of 10 pounds for 75 minutes or pressure for 85 minutes if using quart jars.

7. When canner has depressurized, allow jars to cool for 10 minutes before removing them from the pressure canner. Place the jars on a towel on the counter and leave them undisturbed for 12 hours. Store in a cool, dark place.

BOSTON BAKED BEANS

This is a great recipe of beans. Be sure to remove as much of the fat from the beef as you can so that your mixture is safe for storage. Salt is not necessary for preserving canned foods, it is used for flavor and can be lessened or eliminated if you like. Recipe makes 5 pints.

INGREDIENTS:

- 3 cups of navy beans
- 6 slices of bacon, diced
- 3 to 4 tbsp. of molasses
- 1 tbsp. of salt
- 1 tbsp. mustard seeds, ground
- ½ cup of barbecue sauce or tomato ketchup
- ¼ to ½ cup of raw cane or brown sugar
- 1 medium sweet onion, diced
- 4 to 5 tsp. of Worcestershire sauce
- ½ tbsp. of crushed black pepper, or as needed to taste
- 3 cups of water per 1 cup of beans

DIRECTIONS:

1. Sort the beans and discard damaged beans. Rinse the beans with water and drain in a colander. In a large stock pot add the beans and 9 cups of water. Apply medium-high heat, cover with the lid and bring to a boil. Boil for 2 minutes and remove the pot from heat. Let it stand in the pot for 1 hour with lid on. Drain and rinse beans, set aside.
2. Return the beans into the stock pot and pour in 9 more cups of water. Apply medium-high heat and bring to a boil. Drain the beans with a colander and reserve the cooking liquid.

3. Combine together the bacon, molasses, salt, ground mustard, ketchup, brown sugar, onion, Worcestershire sauce, pepper and 4 cups of the reserved cooking liquid in the same stock pot. Apply medium-high heat and bring to a boil. Remove from heat and stir in the drained beans. Adjust consistency according to preference by adding more cooking liquid.
4. Place the mixture in a preheated oven at 350 °F and bake for about 3 to 4 hours. Stir the mixture every hour and adding more bean water if necessary to adjust the consistency. After 2 hours of baking, taste beans and adjust seasonings according to preferred taste. Bake for another 1 to 2 hours and remove from the oven.
5. Ladle beans into the prepared canning jars and add more cooking liquid to cover 1 inch above the beans. Cover jars with lids and rings and wipe clean. Process with for 65 minutes at 10 pounds of pressure.
6. Remove pressure canner from heat, allow pressure to release on its own and lower in temperature. Remove the jars when completely cool and let it stand for 24 hours undisturbed.

Kidney Beans

Dried beans take quite a while to cook, making them an inconvenient option when time is tight. Countless meals have been derailed by forgetting to put the beans to soak the night before. That's why so many people buy commercially canned beans. Some buy them exclusively, never cooking dried beans at all. Others buy them as a backup plan in the event of a dried bean failure or for the occasional quick and convenient meal. Dried beans are still the better bargain cost-wise and canning your own beans is fairly simple. It's nice to have canned beans on the shelf. You can open a jar to bulk up a pot of soup, perhaps use one to make a single pot dish like chicken, red beans and rice, or some other fast but healthy meal. With this recipe, it is easy to make as many or as few pints or quarts as you like. You add salt to the individual jar, rather than to the entire batch.

INGREDIENTS:

4 cups of dried kidney beans, soaked for at least 12 hours

1 tsp. of salt

Water, as needed to cover the beans

DIRECTIONS:

1. Pick through the dried beans, removing any stones, clots of dirt, or other debris and any shriveled, misshapen or otherwise bad beans. Wash beans in a colander under cold running water, and then put them in a heavy stainless steel pot. Add enough cold water to cover, put the lid on the pot and put in a cool place for 12 to 18 hours.

2. After the beans have soaked, bring them to a boil over medium-high heat. Reduce heat to medium and let them boil for 30 minutes, adjusting temperature as needed to keep them at a boil.

3. While the beans boil, set up the pressure canner and sterilize the necessary jars and lids. Keep them sterile by leaving them in simmering, not boiling, water until you're ready to use them.

4. When the beans have boiled for 30 minutes, turn off the heat and pack the hot beans into the hot, sterile jars. Allow a 1-inch head space. If desired, add 1 tsp. of salt to each quart jar. Use ½ tsp. of salt in each pint jar.

5. Pour boiling water over beans, maintaining each jar's 1-inch headspace. Top with hot lids, then tighten rings. Process quart jars in pressure canner for 90 minutes at 10 pounds of pressure and pints, also at 10 pounds of pressure, for 75 minutes.

6. Once the pressure canner has been depressurized and vented, remove jars and set them on a towel to cool. Let them sit, undisturbed, for at least 12 hours, then check seals. Put correctly sealed jars in a cool, dark place for up to 12 months. A poorly sealed jar must be stored in the refrigerator. Use the beans within 3 days.

Salsa

Tomatillo Green Salsa

This savory, spicy hot green salsa is made with fresh tomatillos, with plenty of green chilies and jalapeño peppers to turn up the heat. Onion, garlic and spices temper that heat, adding a depth and fullness of flavor that is well complemented by the tart tang of the lemon. This is a quick and simple canning project, ideal for the beginner getting a feel for the hot water bath canning method. These jars do not have to be sterilized prior to filling because they will be processed for longer than 10 minutes. However, as always, they should be scrupulously clean.

Makes: 5 pints of salsa.

INGREDIENTS:

- 5 cups chopped tomatillos
- 1 1/2 cups seeded, chopped long green chiles
- 1/2 cup fine chopped jalapeño peppers, seeds removed
- 4 cups chopped red onions
- 1 cup bottled lemon juice
- 6 cloves garlic, finely chopped
- 1 tbsp. ground cumin
- 3 tbsp. oregano leaves
- 1 tbsp. salt
- 1 tsp. black pepper

DIRECTIONS:

1. In a large saucepan, stir together all ingredients, then place pan over high heat. Bring the saucepan to a boil while stirring often. Lower the heat and allow ingredients in the saucepan to simmer for 20 minutes, stirring frequently.

2. While hot, use a ladle to fill the pint jars, allowing for ½ inch of headspace. Put the lids and rings on the jars, then use your All American® to process the pint jars in boiling water for 15 minutes at an altitude up to 1,000 feet. For altitudes between 1,001 and 6,000 feet, process 20 minutes and 25 minutes for altitudes over 6,000 feet.

3. When processing is complete, remove the jars carefully and place on a counter that has been covered in a towel. Allow to cool overnight. Check to make sure jars sealed properly and store in a cool, dark place.

BLACK BEAN AND CORN SALSA

This recipe is really versatile as it could easily be used as a chili or soup. You can add more peppers to make it spicier or use dry spices for a smoky essence. This recipe can bulked up with additional vegetables for a more chunky dip. Don't sweat it if you don't have any Epazote seasoning in your cupboard, but you'll love it when you give it a try!

INGREDIENTS:

1 ½ cups onions, chopped

6 cloves garlic, diced

1 tbsp. Epazote seasoning

1 tsp. red chili flakes

1/3 cup vinegar

2 cups black beans

2 cups Corn

4 cups tomatoes, chopped

1 cup Jalapeno pepper, chopped

1 tsp. black pepper

1 tbsp. cilantro, dried

1 tbsp. Kosher salt

2 cups tomato sauce

DIRECTIONS:

1. Sort and soak beans overnight. Drain beans and put them in a pot with 4 cups of water. Keep flame low and do not boil as to avoid beans splitting. Simmer for 30 minutes.
2. Gently drain beans so as not to mash them. Reserve liquid and put aside. Return beans to pot along with all remaining ingredients. Toss gently and cook for 10 minutes. Put prepared jars on a clean dish towel. Then put salsa into jars, leaving 1 inch of headspace. Use reserved bean liquid if you desire a bit thinner salsa. Make sure there are no air bubbles. Wipe the rims and lids of the jars.
3. Close lid and bring to a boil then allow steam to vent for 10 minutes. Close vent and pressure at 10 lbs for 85 minutes. If you are using pint sized jars pressure at 10 lbs.
4. After canner has depressurized, remove the jars from the canner placing them on a towel in a safe spot to sit undisturbed for at least 12 hours. Check seals and store in a cool, dark place to be used within a year.

Peach Salsa

This flavorful salsa complements simple grilled or broiled fish nicely. It can also be used in place of your usual salsa with chips, tacos and other Tex-Mex type foods. Take the extra couple minutes to fresh grind the cumin seeds in a pestle and mortar instead of using prepackaged and already ground. It really makes a difference in terms of flavor. A colorful salsa, it looks quite pretty in the glass canning jars, making it a great choice for gift-giving during the holiday season. A bit of summer captured in a sun-ripened peach is always welcome during the cold season. This recipe makes eight 1/2-pint jars of sweet and spicy salsa.

Ingredients:

- 3 lbs. peaches
- 3 large fresh tomatoes
- 1 1/2 cups chopped red onions
- 4 medium jalapeño peppers, seeds removed and chopped finely
- 1 large red bell pepper, seeds removed and chopped finely
- 1/2 cup fresh cilantro, chopped finely
- 1/2 cup white vinegar
- 2 tbsp. honey
- 3 cloves garlic, chopped finely
- 1 1/2 tsp. freshly ground cumin seeds
- 1/2 tsp. cayenne pepper

Directions:

1. Sterilize 8 ½-pint jars and lids. Leave them in the hot water until you're ready to use them.

2. Blanch peaches, then plunge them into cold water to cool. Remove skins and pits, then chop. Blanch tomatoes, slip skins off, then remove the seeds and coarsely chop into chunks.

3. In a big stainless steel pot, stir together peaches, jalapeño peppers, onion, tomatoes, red bell pepper, honey, vinegar, cilantro, garlic, cayenne and cumin. Bring to boiling, then cook 5 minutes, while stirring often.

4. If it is still a bit thin or soupy at the 5 minute mark, boil it for just a few more minutes until it thickens up some. Adjust seasonings, adding a bit more cayenne if you'd like it spicier.

5. Spoon hot salsa into the hot jars, leaving ¼ of an inch of headspace at the top. Use your rubber spatula to remove any air bubbles in jars, making sure to maintain that 1/4-inch headspace. With a damp paper towel, wipe jar threads and rims, making sure that there is nothing to interfere with jar sealing.

6. Put the lids on and tighten rings. Process the jars in the All American® for approximately 10 minutes under 10 pounds pressure.

7. Remove the jars from the canner carefully, without sloshing or jostling the contents, and put onto a towel on the counter to cool. Leave the jars undisturbed for 24 hours, then check to make sure the jars have sealed properly.

8. Store correctly sealed jars in a cool, dark and happy place for up to 12 months. Store any that didn't seal as they should have in the refrigerator and use within a week.

Pineapple Mango Salsa

This fruity salsa is not only perfect for chips and crackers, it makes dressing up a plain 'ole chicken breast a snap. Substitute this Hawaiian inspired salsa in your favorite Salsa Chicken recipe for a fresh take on an old favorite. My wife likes to serve this salsa with cinnamon pita chips when we have company. Recipe makes 4 pints.

Ingredients:

4 cups diced tomatoes

3 cups chopped pineapple

2 mangoes, peeled and diced

1 cup sweet onion, finely chopped

1 cup red bell pepper, finely chopped

2 jalapeño pepper, finely chopped

1/3 cup sugar

1/4 cup lime juice

1/4 cup cider vinegar

1 tsp. grated ginger

2 cloves minced garlic

1/2 tsp salt

Directions:

1. In a large, heavy non-reactive pot combine all the ingredients and stir. Bring the mixture to a boil, then lower the heat. Simmer for 10 minutes, with the lid off. Stir several times while mixture simmers.
2. After about 10 minutes, remove the salsa from heat. Ladle the salsa into prepared pint sized jars while it is still hot. Be sure to leave 1/2

inch of headspace. Remove any air bubbles with a plastic knife. Wipe the jars and rims clean. Apply the lids and tighten the rings.

3. Place closed jars into your All American® canner. Make sure there is enough water in the pot to cover the jars by 1-2 inches. Process at a full rolling boil for 20 min.

4. When jars have boiled for 20 minutes, remove from heat. Carefully remove jars from canner and place on a towel covered counter. Cool for at least 12 hours before checking to be sure that jars have sealed properly. Store in a cool, dark place.

SPICY SALSA

This is a classic spicy tomato salsa that you will enjoy using for chips and tacos. Years ago, I used to chop all the vegetables by hand, but lately I've been putting my food processor to work. The food processor will make the veggies pretty small, so if you enjoy a chunkier salsa, either process minimally or hand chop. Makes 5 pints and the recipe doubles well.

INGREDIENTS:

7 cups diced tomatoes

1 1/2 cups chopped onion

1 1/2 cups green peppers

8 jalapeños, seeded and finely chopped

3 cloves minced garlic

1 can tomato paste (6 ounces)

3/4 cup white vinegar

1 tsp. ground cumin

2 tsp. salt

1 1/2 tsp pepper

1 1/2 tsp oregano

1-2 tsp cayenne pepper (to taste)

DIRECTIONS:

1. In a large, non-reactive pot add all the ingredients and give them a quick stir. Bring the mixture to a boil, stirring consistently. When salsa reaches a boil, reduce heat and allow to simmer for 30 minutes. Stir frequently so salsa does not scorch or stick to the bottom of the pot.
2. Remove the salsa from heat and ladle the hot mixture into prepared pint jars. Leave 1/2 inch of headspace. Use a plastic knife to remove any air bubbles and wipe the jars and rims with a clean cloth. Apply the lids and tighten the rings.
3. Place jars into the prepared All American canner. Be sure to have 1-2 inches of water covering the tops of the jars. Bring the water back to a boil and begin the timer when the water has reached a full, rolling boil. Process for 20 minutes at a boil.
4. After 20 minutes, remove the canner from the heat source. Allow to sit in the canner for a few minutes before removing and placing on a towel covered counter or table to cool. Cool for at least 12 hours before checking the seals on the jars.

5

Jellies, Jams, & Marmalades

Country Meadow Dandelion Jelly

This lovely, golden jelly is made with sun-drenched, country meadow dandelion blossoms. It is important not to use city dandelions. The gritty toughness and fierce drive to survive of the city dandelion, the ability to grow and blossom even in a crack in a sidewalk, is truly admirable. However, city dandelions, even those growing in the park, absorb chemicals from vehicle exhaust fumes, lawn pesticide sprays and other environmental contaminants. Use dandelions from a wild meadow, one that isn't sprayed for insects or weeds and is far away from motor traffic. You need just the blossoms, not the stems, for this jelly. This recipe makes four or five ½-pint jars.

Ingredients:

- 10 cups dandelion blossoms
- 3 cups dandelion tea (use above blossoms to make tea)
- 4 ½ cups sugar
- 2 tbsp. lemon juice
- 1 box powdered pectin

Directions:

1. Using a sharp, small pair of scissors, snip the green base off the bottom of each dandelion blossom, pulling away the other green parts with your fingers. Drop the yellow petals into a 4-cup glass measure. After working through the 10 cups of blossoms, there should be about 4 cups of dandelion petals. Pour boiling water over petals, cover and let steep overnight.
2. After the petals are finished steeping, pour the dandelion tea through a fine meshed sieve. Discard the petals and rinse the sieve. Line the sieve with a coffee filter or paper towel and pour the dandelion tea through again. Measure 3 cups of the dandelion tea and set aside.

3. Set up the All American®, making sure to fill it deep enough to cover the jars by at least an inch or two of water. Sterilize jars and lids. Keep them in hot water until they are needed.

4. Combine the 3 cups dandelion tea, the lemon juice and the powdered pectin in a heavy stainless steel saucepan. Bring to boiling over medium heat. Stir in the sugar, then let the pan come to a boil again. Boil for 1 to 2 minutes, then pour into the sterilized hot jars, leaving ¼ inch of headspace.

5. Wipe the rims and threads of the jars with a damp cloth. Put on the lids and tighten the rings. Process in the All American® using boiling water (at a full, rolling boil) for 10 minutes. After processing is complete, remove from canner and set to cool on a towel spread on the counter or table. Let the jars sit, without being disturbed, for at least 12 hours.

6. After the cooling and resting period is done, check to see if the jars sealed properly. Well sealed jars can be stored for up to 1 year in a cool, dark spot. If a jar didn't seal as it should have, store it in the refrigerator.

Cabernet Wine Jelly

I'm getting' fancy with this one! Show off this jelly at a special occasion by pairing with brie or soft goat cheese. Choose a good bottle of wine (doesn't have to be expensive) and combine with simple ingredients to create a jelly you will be making over and over again. Cabernet wines are bold and rich in flavor and are the most widely produced type of wine. Recipe makes 4 half-pints.

Ingredients:

- 3 cups Cabernet wine
- ½ tsp. Lemon juice
- 3 ½ cups sugar
- 6 oz liquid pectin

Directions:

1. Pour wine into a large pot and heat over a high flame. Bring to a boil and add sugar and lemon juice. Stir to combine and cook for 5 minutes. Put in pectin, stir and remove from flame.
2. Ladle jelly into prepared jars, leaving 1/2 inch headspace. Remove any air bubbles, wipe the rims of the jars and lids with a clean cloth and fasten lids.
3. Place into the All American® and process for 15 minutes at full rolling boil. Make sure water covers the lids by at least 1-2 inches. Turn off the heat, remove cover and allow jars to sit in the pot for a few minutes. Remove from canner and place on a dish towel for a day and allow to cool.

Jalapeño Jelly

Sweet with heat, this spicy jelly has been garnering a lot of attention. Jalapeño jelly started out as a local culinary quirk, then became a regional favorite. Now, it seems to be showing up on or next to all kinds of foods. Try it as a glaze for pork chops, ham and chicken wings. Serve it as a dip with coconut fried shrimp, jalapeño poppers, sweet potato fries and deep-fried vegetables, including okra, zucchini, and eggplant. Use it on sandwiches, like a ham, egg and cheese on a bagel. Spread it on cornbread, on crackers topped with cheese and on apple slices.

Makes: 4 pints

Ingredients:

- 1 large red bell pepper
- 1 large green bell pepper
- 10 jalapeño peppers
- 1 ½ cups white vinegar
- ½ tsp. salt
- 5 to 6 cups granulated sugar
- 3 ounces liquid fruit pectin

Directions:

1. Put enough water into your All American® to cover the filled pint jars by at least an inch. Bring the water in the canner to a boil, then lower the heat and keep the water at a simmer. Wash, rinse and sterilize 4 pint jars and their lids. Leave the jars and lids in simmering water until needed.

2. Fine chop the bell peppers and the jalapeños, then put them in a large, heavy-bottomed pot. Add the vinegar, salt and sugar. Stir to combine well. Bring the pot to boiling and allow to boil for 10 minutes, stirring

frequently. Pour in the liquid pectin, boil for another minute and remove from heat.

3. Leaving ¼ inch head-space, carefully pour hot jelly into hot, sterilized jars. Use a damp paper towel to wipe jar rims and threads. Top each jar with its lid and tighten each ring. Place the jars on the canner rack and bring the canner to a boil. Process the jars for 10 minutes. Carefully remove the jars from the All American® and set them in a secure spot to cool. Let the jelly sit undisturbed for a day or two to set-up properly.

Pepper Jelly

Pepper jelly is a condiment that goes great with meats and can also be paired with cream cheese and eaten with crackers. Pepper jelly has a mixture of sweet and spicy flavors. This recipe uses pectin in the powdered form; do not replace with any other form of pectin. Powdered pectin can be added to raw fruits or juice but liquid pectin has to be added after mixture is boiled. Recipe makes 6 pints.

Ingredients:

8 large sweet green peppers, seeded and diced

½ cup of cider vinegar

4 tbsp. of liquid Pectin

3 cups of sugar

1 medium Jalapeño pepper, seeded

½ cup of apple juice

½ tsp. of table salt

DIRECTIONS:

1. Place the diced green bell peppers, jalapeño and cider vinegar in a blender and puree until smooth or into a coarse mixture if preferred.

2. Transfer the puree into a pot and add in the apple juice. Apply medium-high heat and boil for about 10 minutes while stirring regularly. Stir in the liquid pectin, salt and sugar and boil until the sugar is completely dissolved. Remove pot from heat and set aside.

3. Spoon the jelly into the prepared jars leaving ¼ inch of headspace. Wipe the rims and lids of the jars with a clean cloth and tightly close the lids. Place into the prepared All American® pressure canner and process for 10 minutes at a rolling boil.

4. Carefully remove jars from the canner and place on a towel on a table or counter. Allow to cool for 12-24 hours. Check seals and store properly sealed jars in a cool, dark place.

Carrot Jam

This fragrant, lightly spiced jam is a delicious complement to roasted and braised game meats. The taste of the wild, that certain fullness of flavor common to venison, duck and other wild-caught game, is well accented by the richly aromatic dessert spices used in this jam. Put this jam on the table when having a late afternoon tea with cold meats and thick slices of pumpernickel bread, toasted nice and hot. It is lovely on delicate, well-bred and civilized breads, but this jam truly comes into its own on a good, dark and strong peasant bread. Use a pestle and mortar to grind your spices right before using for the best flavor. This recipe makes between six and seven 1/2-pint jars.

Ingredients:

4 cups grated carrots

3 cups sugar

2 lemons, grate rind and extract juice

½ tsp. ground cloves

½ tsp. ground allspice

½ tsp. ground cinnamon

Directions:

1. Combine all ingredients in a large, heavy-bottomed stainless steel pot. Bring to a boil over medium-high heat. Lower heat to medium-low and let simmer, stirring all the while, until thick.
2. Pour the hot jam into hot, sterilized jars. Carefully wipe each jar's rim and threads with a damp clean cloth or paper towel. Put the lids on, tighten rings and process in the All American® for 10 minutes with water at a full boil.
3. After processing is complete, remove from canner to a towel spread on the counter to cool. Let the jars sit, undisturbed, for a minimum of 12 hours, then check seals.

4. Store well sealed jars in a cool, dark place for up to 12 months. If a jar doesn't seal the way it should, store it in the refrigerator and use soon.

BANANA-ORANGE JAM

This is a delightful jam to use at teatime (or if Downton Abbey is on), with neat little scones just out of the oven or freshly toasted English muffins. Use it to make peanut butter and jam sandwiches on honey whole wheat bread. You'll need to pay close attention while cooking this jam down to avoid scorching. Make sure you have everything you need within reach, because it's best not to turn your back for an instant with this one. This recipe makes about eight ½-pint jars.

INGREDIENTS:

12 cups sliced bananas

1 ½ cups orange juice

3 strips orange peel

2 cinnamon sticks

6 cups sugar

¾ cup lemon juice

6 strips lemon peel

6 whole cloves

Directions:

1. In a large, heavy-bottomed stainless steel pot, combine all ingredients. Put the pot over medium heat and cook, stirring constantly, until sugar dissolves. Bring the pot to boiling and hold it at a hard boil for 10 minutes, stirring to avoid sticking or scorching.

2. Drop the temperature down to low and let the pot simmer, while stirring continuously, for 20 minutes or until the jam is thick. Remove the pot from heat. Use a spoon to take out the fruit peels, cinnamon sticks and whole cloves.

3. Fill the hot, sterile jars with the hot jam, leaving ½ inch of headspace. Carefully wipe jar rims and threads, put the lids on and tighten rings. Process in the All American® for 20 minutes at a rolling boil.

4. Remove from canner to a towel on the counter or table to cool. Let jars sit undisturbed for a minimum of 12 hours, then check seals.

5. Store properly sealed jars in a cool, dark place for up to 12 months. If a jar has a bad seal, then it must be stored in the refrigerator and used soon.

APRICOT MANGO JAM

Apricot and mango complement each other in this simple jam. The aroma of the mango goes well with the chunks of apricot and can be paired with yogurt. I'm a mango maniac but hate dicing them as that core can be a pain to cut around. It's worth it. Other types of pectin may be used when making your jam, just be sure to pay close attention to the amount to be used by each varied brand. Recipe makes 6 pints.

INGREDIENTS:

- 2 cup mangoes, chopped
- ¼ cups lemon juice
- 4 cups apricots, pitted and diced
- 1 cup sugar
- 3 tbsp. Pectin, ball

DIRECTIONS:

1. Put mangoes and apricots into a large Dutch oven and cook for 15 minutes over a medium flame, stirring frequently to avoid burning. When mangoes have gotten mushy put in lemon juice and sugar and stir for 5 minutes until sugar dissolves.
2. Bring mixture to a boil then add pectin, stir and boil for one minute. Take pot from heat.
3. Use a ladle or spoon to put jam into prepared jars, leaving ¼ inch headspace. Wipe the rims of the jars and lids with a clean cloth and fasten lids. Place into the All American® and process for 10 minutes at a full rolling boil.
4. Remove from canner and place on a dish towel undisturbed and allow to cool.

5. If jars make a popping sound that means they are cooling and sealing. Check seals and reseal any unsealed jar. Store until needed.

Blackberry Jam

Fresh blackberries are a pretty high dollar grocery store item in most places. However, with a little creativity, this doesn't have to be a high dollar jam. In many regions, blackberry bushes grow like weeds, easily found around lakes and streams and in lightly wooded places. It's not just rural areas either. City parks, old cemeteries, foreclosed and abandoned homes, bike paths – these are just some of the locations that blackberry bushes may be found. Wild blackberries seem to taste so much more real than do their bland grocery store counterparts.

Makes: 4 - 8-ounce jars.

Ingredients:

- 3 cups blackberries crushed with a potato masher
- 4 cups sugar
- 1 ounce dry pectin

Directions:

1. Fill your All American® with enough water to cover the filled and closed jars by at least an inch. Bring the water to a boil, then reduce the heat and hold the water at a simmer. Wash, rinse and sterilize 4 8-ounce jars and their lids. Leave the jars and lids in the hot water until they are needed.
2. Put the blackberries into a large heavy-bottomed saucepan. Stir in the pectin, adding it slowly. Put the pan over high heat and, stirring constantly, add the sugar all at once. Continue stirring, bring to a boil and hold it there a moment. Remove the saucepan from heat.
3. Ladle the hot blackberries into hot, sterile jars, allowing for a ½ inch head-space. Use a damp paper towel to wipe jar rims and threads,

then put the lids on and tighten the rings. Put the jars on the canner rack, adding more water if needed to cover the jars by an inch.

4. Bring the All American® to a boil and process jars for 10 minutes. Carefully take the jars out of the canner and put on a towel to cool for 12 hours.

Pina Colada Jam

A creative way to flavor your jams is by making them taste like your favorite drinks. Party jam! Since we want avoid cream in our canned goods, the coconut cream is replaced with coconut flavored liquor. Recipe makes 4 half-pints.

Ingredients:

- 3 cups pineapple, crushed
- ¼ cup lime juice
- 2 cups sugar
- ½ cup orange juice
- 3 tbsp. classic pectin
- ½ cup coconut rum

Directions:

1. Prepare canning equipment. Set up the canning equipment or a pot large enough to hold jars, sterilize jars and lids, and keep them in hot water until ready to use.
2. Combine orange juice, coconut liquor, pineapple and lime juice in a large pot. Stir then add pectin.
3. Place pot over a high flame and bring to a full boil (a boil that cannot be stirred down). Put in sugar and stir until dissolved; boil again for one minute.
4. Remove from flame and use a ladle or spoon to put jam into prepared jars, leaving ¼ inch headspace. Remove any air bubbles. Wipe the rims of the jars and lids with a clean cloth and fasten lids.
5. Place into the All American® and process for 10 minutes at full rolling boil. Be sure water is covering the tops of the jars by at least an inch or two.

6. When processing is complete, remove cover and allow jars to sit in the pot for a few minutes. Remove from canner and place on a dish towel and allow to cool over night.
7. If jars make a popping sound that means they are cooling and sealing. Check seals and reseal any unsealed jar. Store until needed.

RHUBARB CONSERVE

There is more to rhubarb than just pie. Of course, rhubarb pie is a delectable treat any day of the week. There's no doubt about that. However, rhubarb is also delicious when made into a conserve. While some people do like to use the conserve like a jam, spreading it on fluffy, hot biscuits right out of the oven, it also goes wonderfully with meat. Serve this rhubarb conserve with pork, rabbit and poultry. This recipe makes about five 1/2-pint jars.

INGREDIENTS:

1 1/4 lbs. rhubarb, chopped

1 large orange, in paper-thin slices

1/2 large lemon, in paper-thin slices

4 cups sugar

1/4 cup coarsely chopped pecans

2 tbsp. golden raisins

1/4 tsp. ground cloves

Directions:

1. Remove seeds from orange slices and cut each paper-thin slice into 6 or 8 small wedges. In a large, heavy stainless steel saucepan, combine the rhubarb, orange, lemon and sugar over medium heat, then bring to a boil. Reduce heat to low and simmer uncovered, stirring often, for 40 minutes.
2. While the rhubarb simmers, set up the All American®. Sterilize the jars and lids. Keep them sterile by leaving them in hot, almost simmering water until ready to use.
3. After the rhubarb has simmered for 40 minutes, add the pecans, raisins and ground cloves. Simmer for another 5 minutes.
4. Pour hot rhubarb mixture into hot, sterile jars, leaving ¼ inch of headspace. With a damp cloth or paper towel, carefully wipe the rim and threads of each jar. Place the lids on the jars, then tighten the rings.
5. Carefully arrange the jars in the All American®. Process the jars for 15 minutes once the water has reached a full, rolling boil.
6. Turn off the heat source. Remove lid from pressure canner and carefully remove the jars. Place jars on a clean towel and let them sit overnight undisturbed.

STRAWBERRY LEMON MARMALADE

If you don't have any fresh strawberries around, I'm sorry. That's a sad day round these parts. We love to go picking fresh strawberries and will often end up with pounds and pounds of them. They go bad pretty quickly when they're fresh. Can em up! Recipe makes 4 half-pints.

INGREDIENTS:

- 4 lemons, chopped
- 3 cups water
- 1 quart strawberries in sugar
- 3 cups sugar

DIRECTIONS:

1. Prepare canning equipment. Sterilize jars and lids, and keep them in hot water until ready to use.
2. Slice lemons as thin as you can then dice slices. Put them into a pot and cover with water, cook for 5 minutes over a low flame. Remove from heat and cover.
3. Crush the berries and add them to the pot. Add sugar and stir. Heat until mixture begins to boil; boil until mixture becomes gel like.
4. Use a ladle or spoon to put jam into prepared jars, leaving ¼ inch headspace.
5. Wipe the rims of the jars and lids with a clean cloth and fasten the lids. Place into the All American® and process for 10 minutes at full rolling boil. Remove from canner and place on a dish towel undisturbed and allow to cool.
6. If jars make a popping sound that means they are cooling and sealing. Check seals and reseal any unsealed jar. Store until needed.

Citrus Trifecta Marmalade

This is a pretty marmalade, made with pink grapefruit, navel oranges and limes. As lovely as it looks in the glass canning jars, it tastes even better, a perfect balance between sweet and tart with the slightest, most delicate hint of bitter. Serve it with hot scones or biscuits and you'll notice, with the warmth of the bread, how deliciously fragrant this marmalade is. It also goes well with a rich, creamy mildly flavored soft cheese on whole grain crackers, thinly sliced dark pumpernickel or puffy, warm Mediterranean style pita breads. This recipe makes six 1/2-pint jars.

Ingredients:

- 8 navel oranges
- 6 limes
- 4 pink grapefruit
- 12 cups water
- 12 cups of sugar
- 8 cups of zest cooking liquid

Directions:

1. Thoroughly wash and dry oranges, limes and grapefruits. Carefully trim the zest from the citrus peels in strips. With a sharp paring knife, cut those strips of zest thinner and thinner until they look as though they've been finely shredded.

2. Put the zest in a heavy stainless steel pot. Pour 12 cups of water over the zest. Put the pot over high heat and bring to boiling. Decrease the temperature to medium-high and let the pot simmer for 30 minutes.

3. While the pot simmers, remove the pith, membranes and seeds from the fruit. Put the citrus fruit sections, without their membranes, in a glass or stainless steel bowl and set aside. Collect the pith, membranes

and seeds, then tie them securely in a clean, double-layered square of cheesecloth.

4. After the zest has simmered for 30 minutes, pour the contents of the pot through a sieve set over a glass or stainless steel bowl. Let the zest drain thoroughly. Measure and set aside 8 cups of the zest's cooking liquid.

5. Stir together the zest, the fruit, the 8 cups of reserved zest cooking liquid and the 12 cups of sugar in a large, heavy-bottomed stainless steel or enamelware pot. Add pith, membranes and seeds tightly tied in cheesecloth.

6. Put the pot over medium-high heat and bring to a boil. Let the pot boil for 30 to 40 minutes or until the contents of the pot reach 220 degrees Fahrenheit. Hold that temperature for 1 full minute, then take the pot off the heat.

7. While the pot boils, set up the All American®. Fill it with enough water to cover the filled jars by a depth of at least an inch or two. Sterilize jars and lids. Hold the sterile jars and lids in almost simmering hot water until it is time to fill them.

8. Immediately after removing the marmalade pot from heat, stir for a minute or two to distribute the zest evenly throughout. Ladle the hot marmalade into the hot jars, leaving 1/2 inch of headspace. With a clean, damp lint-free cloth, carefully wipe jar rims and threads. Put on the lids and tighten the rings.

9. Put the jars in the All American®, being sure water covers the jars by about 2 inches. Process for 10 minutes at a full boil. After processing, remove the jars from the canner and put them on a towel-lined counter or table to cool. Let sit undisturbed for at least 12 hours, then check seals.

10. Store correctly sealed jars in a cool, dark spot for up to 1 year. If a can doesn't seal properly, store that one in the refrigerator. Try to use it within a few weeks.

BLUEBERRY ORANGE MARMALADE

Blueberries are a super food and canning them well is a super power. Making fresh marmalade ensures you know exactly what you are eating. There is no need for pectin in this mix however it could be added if so desired. Recipe makes 5 half-pints.

INGREDIENTS:

- 1 Orange
- 2 cups water
- 2 cups fresh blueberries
- 1 lemon
- 2 ½ cups sugar
- 1 cinnamon stick

DIRECTIONS:

1. Squeeze orange and lemon into a bowl and remove any seeds from juice. Slice remaining rind thinly and add to pot with cinnamon and water, bring to a boil then lower heat and cook for 25 minutes until rind is tender.
2. Remove cinnamon and add citrus juice and blueberries.
3. Cover pot and cook for 15 minutes at a rolling boil. Stir in sugar and leave uncovered. Cook until mixture becomes gel like.
4. Use a ladle or spoon to put jam into prepared jars, leaving 1/2 inch headspace. Wipe the rims of the jars and lids with a clean cloth and fasten lids.
5. Place into All American® and process for 10 minutes at full rolling boil. After processing is complete, remove from canner and set to cool on a towel spread on the counter or table. Let the jars sit, without being disturbed, for at least 12 hours.

6. After the cooling and resting period is done, check to see if the jars sealed properly. Well sealed jars can be stored for up to 1 year in a cool, dark spot. If a jar didn't seal as it should have, store it in the refrigerator.

BLOOD ORANGE MARMALADE

The blood oranges that give this marmalade its vibrant hue were first officially recorded in Italy during the 1600s. Some evidence suggests that blood oranges were cultivated in Sicily as early as the 9th or 10th century, when the region was under Arabic rule. The blood oranges introduced by the Arabs may have originated in China, moving west along trade routes. There are several varieties of blood orange. Many are sweeter than the more commonplace orange varieties, with a stronger, more intensely orange fragrance and flavor. Some, like the Moro, also known for its distinctively sweet, raspberry tinged flavor, have deeply red flesh that ranges from blood red to deep ruby to a crimson so dark that it is almost black in color. Not all varieties have such intense color. Some, such as the Tarocco, the orange variety with the highest concentration of Vitamin C, have flesh with a lighter blush of red.

Makes: 7 half-pint jars.

INGREDIENTS:

4 lbs. blood oranges

3 tbsp. fresh lemon juice

4 cups sugar

DIRECTIONS:

1. Remove the peel from 3 or 4 oranges with a vegetable peeler, then use a sharp paring knife to trim away any white pith remaining on the peel. Cut the peel into paper thin slices and set aside. Peel the rest of the oranges, also removing white membranes and seeds, then cut oranges into small cubes.

2. Over medium-high heat, bring the orange pieces, lemon juice and sugar to a boil in a 3-quart saucepan, stirring often. When it boils, lower heat to medium and let simmer for about 45 minutes or a candy thermometer hits 225 degrees F.

3. Prepare the All American® as a boiling water canner, filling with enough water to cover the filled and capped jars by at least an inch. Bring the water to a boil, then reduce heat and let the canner simmer. Wash, rinse and sterilize 7 half-pint jars and their lids. Leave the jars and lids in hot water until ready to use.

4. Put the orange peel slices in a small saucepan, then cover with water. Heat the saucepan to a boil. Let it simmer for about 4 minutes, then drain.

5. During the last few minutes of the orange mixture's simmering time, stir the orange peel slices into the orange mixture. Spoon the marmalade into clean, sterile jars. Use a clean, damp towel to wipe jar rims and threads. Put lids on the jars and tighten the rings.

6. Place the jars on the canner rack. Add water, if necessary to ensure that the jars are covered by at least an inch of water. Bring the All American® to a boil and process the jars for 10 minutes once the water reaches a full boil. Take the jars out of the canner and set them to cool where they will not be disturbed. Check the jar seals after 24 hours.

6

Spreads, Chutney, & Relishes

APRICOT HONEY BUTTER

This recipe uses dried fruits so it takes some patience and time to allow the apricots to cook until tender. The sage honey and ginger infuse the apricots and make this spread perfect. Recipe makes 3 half-pints.

INGREDIENTS:

- 2 cups apricots, dried and chopped
- 2 cups water
- ¼ cup crystallized ginger
- 2 tbsp. lemon zest
- 2/3 cups sage honey
- ½ cup lemon juice

DIRECTIONS:

1. Put apricots, ginger, lemon juice, zest and water in a large Dutch oven. Heat mixture and bring to a boil then lower flame and cook for 30-35 minutes or until apricot gets tender.
2. Remove from heat and put into a food processor, blend until smooth then return to the pot. Add honey and bring to a boil over a medium heat and cook until consistency is gel like.
3. Use a ladle or spoon to put mixture into prepared jars, leaving 1/2 inch headspace.
4. Wipe the rims of the jars and lids with a clean cloth and fasten lids. Place into the All American® and process for 10 minutes once water has reached a rolling boil. Remove and place jars on a clean towel and let them sit overnight undisturbed.
5. Check seals. Store properly sealed jars in a cool, dark place for up to one year. If a jar did not seal properly, it will need to be refrigerated and used.

PAW PAW BUTTER

Why not Maw Maw? Paw Paw isn't my ole granpappy, it's another word for papaya. This tropical fruit is nutritious but does not have a log shelf life. Soft and buttery, can it to indulge in this fruit when it is not in season. You can store and use on fresh breads or pastry or mix with yogurt. Recipe makes 5-6 pints.

INGREDIENTS:

- 5 lbs. Paw paws
- ½ cup lemon juice
- 2 tsp. vanilla extract
- 2 cups water
- 3 cups sugar

DIRECTIONS:

1. Peel paw paws and put into a large pot along with lemon juice and water. You do not need to remove the seeds. Cook over medium heat until paw paws have become soft. When paw paws have softened, press through a sieve.
2. Return paw paw puree to pan and add sugar. Cook over a low flame until mixture gets thick. Remove from heat and add vanilla, stir to combine.
3. Use a ladle or spoon to put mixture into prepared jars, leaving 1/4 inch headspace. Wipe the rims of the jars and lids with a clean cloth and fasten lids.
4. Place into the All American® and process for 10 minutes once water has reached a full boil. Remove jars from water bath and place on a dish towel to cool overnight.

Roasted Red Pepper Spread

This spread can be used in a variety of ways such as a pizza sauce or as a dip. The roasted peppers are robust in flavor but not overpowering. It pairs excellently with pasta or fresh bread. I like to use it as a substitute for ketchup in some recipes. Recipe makes 5 half-pints.

Ingredients:

- 6 lbs. red bell peppers
- 2 cloves garlic
- ½ cup red wine vinegar
- 1 tbsp. sugar
- 1 lb Italian plum tomatoes
- 1 onion, halved
- 1 tsp. salt
- 2 tbsp. Basil, chopped

Directions:

1. Set oven to 425°F. Place tomatoes, onion, peppers and garlic on a greased baking sheet and roast until vegetables have blackened. Take from heat and put tomatoes and pepper into paper bags and set aside to cool. Allow the remaining vegetables to cool.
2. Chop garlic and onion and put aside till needed. Remove seeds from tomatoes and peppers and place into a food processor. Pulse tomatoes and peppers until smooth. You may have to do this in batches.
3. Pour mixture into a large pot along with, onion, basil, salt, garlic, vinegar and sugar. Stir to combine and cook over medium heat for 20 minutes until mixture gets thick.

4. Put mixture into prepared jars, leaving 1/4 inch headspace. Remove any air bubbles, wipe the rims of the jars and lids with a clean cloth and fasten lids. Place into the All American® and process for 10 minutes at full rolling boil. Turn off flame, remove cover and allow jars to sit in the canner for a few more minutes. Remove from canner and place on a dish towel and allow to cool.

PEAR-PERSIMMON CHUTNEY

This can be a feel-good frugal chutney in an adventurous, "cool story, bro" kind of way. That's because you can make this chutney with feral fruits, the fruit of domestic trees left to grow wild. You can find pears and persimmons growing wild on abandoned properties and foreclosed farms, in forgotten corners of old cemeteries and public parks, and in the rich government-controlled lands near lakes, rivers and other waterways. This chutney has a rich flavor, deep and warm, fruity and spicy. Serve it with good cheese, Indian food, grilled meats and braised or roasted game birds. This recipe makes six 1/2-pint jars.

INGREDIENTS:

6 medium to large ripe persimmons

4 medium to large ripe pears

1 medium red onion, minced

2/3 cup firm packed dark brown sugar

1 ½ cups apple cider vinegar

¼ cup grated fresh ginger

¼ cup raisins

2 tsp. salt

1 tsp. allspice

1/8 tsp. ground red pepper

Directions:

1. Wash fruit and cut away any bruises or bad spots. Remove seeds, cores and stems and chop pears and persimmons finely.

2. In a heavy stainless steel pot, combine chopped fruit with minced onion, brown sugar, vinegar, grated ginger, raisins, salt, allspice and ground red pepper. Bring to boil over medium-high heat and cook, stirring frequently, until mixture thickens and the persimmon skins are tender, between 30 and 45 minutes. Watch carefully to avoid scorching.

3. While the chutney simmers, set up the All American®. Put enough water in to cover the filled jars by a depth of at least 1 to 2 inches. Sterilize jars and lids, keeping them in hot, almost simmering water until ready to use.

4. When the chutney is done, ladle the hot chutney into hot jars, leaving ½ inch of headspace. Wipe jar threads and rims with a damp paper towel, then put the lids on and tighten the rings. Process the jars for 10 minutes in the All American® at a rolling boil.

5. After the processing is complete, take the jars out of the canner and put them on a towel to cool completely. Let them sit, undisturbed, for at least 12 hours, then check each jar to make sure it sealed properly.

6. Store well sealed jars in a cool, dark place for up to 1 year. If a jar didn't seal correctly, store it in the refrigerator.

Rhubarb Chutney

As far as chutneys go, rhubarb chutney is more British than it is Indian, one of those dishes brought home from the colonies during the days of empire that evolved over time, eventually becoming British. The sweet aromatic spices, offering just a whisper of Persia and North India, work well with the rhubarb and raisins. The savory flavor of the onions, the cayenne's hint of heat and a tangy apple cider vinegar offer just the right counterpoint to the sweetness of the brown sugar and the raisins. This is a chutney with a complex melody of flavors. Serve it with sharp cheese, cold meats and with pork.

Makes: 5 to 6 pints.

INGREDIENTS:

- 8 cups sliced rhubarb
- 6 cups sliced onion
- 2 cups raisins
- 7 cups light brown sugar
- 4 cups apple cider vinegar
- 2 tbsp. salt
- 2 tsp. cinnamon
- 2 tsp. ginger
- 1 tsp. ground cloves
- 1/4 tsp. cayenne pepper

DIRECTIONS:

1. Wash, rinse and sterilize 6 pint size jars and lids. Leave the jars and lids in hot water until needed. Bring enough water to cover the jars by 1 inch to a boil in the hot water canner. Reduce heat to low to keep the water at a simmer.

2. Stir all ingredients together in a large, heavy-bottomed pot until well mixed, then place over medium heat. Cook, stirring regularly, until the pot boils. Reduce heat and simmer 30 to 45 minutes, stirring often, until the mixture thickens slightly. Keep a close eye on the pot to avoid sticking and scorching.

3. When the chutney reaches your desired degree of thickness, pour it into the jars, leaving ½ inch head-space. With a paper towel or clean damp cloth, wipe rims and threads of jars. Put on the lids and tighten the rings. Use the All American® to process the jars for 10 minutes in boiling water. Remove from canner and set to cool. When jars are completely cool, store in a cool dark place.

Tomato Rhubarb Chutney

What can I say? I can't get enough Rhubarb Chutney! Believe it or not, I was able to whittle my recipes down to two and just had to include them both. Rhubarb has a similar flavor to celery. It blends well with tomatoes and brown sugar in this recipe. This chutney is versatile and can be paired with beef, fish or chicken. Feel free to double the recipe as this only make 3 half pints.

Makes: 3 half pints

Ingredients:

- 1 ½ cups tomatoes, seeds removed and chopped
- 1/3 cup red sweet pepper, chopped
- 1/3 cup vinegar
- ¼ cup brown sugar
- 1 tbsp. lemon juice
- ¼ tsp. Kosher Salt
- 1 cup Rhubarb, fresh and chopped
- 1/3 cup onion, chopped
- 1/3 cup Cranberries, dried
- ¼ cup sugar
- ¼ cup water
- 1 tsp. grated ginger
- 2 cloves garlic, diced

Directions:

1. Put tomatoes, pepper, vinegar, water, ginger, garlic, onion, cranberries, sugars, lemon juice and salt into a large pot, stir to

combine and bring to a boil over medium heat. Cover pot and cook for 25 minutes, stirring frequently.

2. Add rhubarb to mixture, cover and cook for an additional 10 minutes. Remove cover and cook for 5 minutes or until mixture thickens.

3. Use a ladle or spoon to put hot mixture into prepared jars, leaving 1/2 inch of headspace. Remove any air bubbles, wipe the rims of the jars and lids with a clean cloth and fasten lids. Place into the All American® and process for 10 minutes at a full rolling boil.

4. Turn off heat source, remove cover and allow jars to sit in the pot for a few minutes. Remove from canner and place on a dish towel to sit undisturbed and allow to cool.

Corn Relish

Corn relish is a traditional Southern recipe (hey y'all!) and is made from corn kernels seasoned with bell peppers, sugar, and vinegar. Refrigerate a jar after canning to get a burst of flavor from this summer delight. Recipe makes 5 pints.

INGREDIENTS:

- 8 cups corn, fresh
- 1 ½ cups celery, diced
- 1 ½ cups green bell peppers, diced
- 3 cups white vinegar
- 4 tsp. dry mustard
- 2 tsp. celery seed
- 2 cups water
- 1 ½ cups red bell peppers, diced
- 1 cup onion, chopped
- 1 ¾ cups sugar
- 2 tsp. Kosher salt
- 1 tsp. ground turmeric

DIRECTIONS:

1. Put corn into a large pot with water and cook for 5 minutes until slightly tender.
2. Drain and return to pot with celery, onions and bell peppers. Add sugar, salt, turmeric, vinegar, mustard and celery seed; stir to combine and cook until sugar dissolves.

3. Ladle corn relish into prepared jars, leaving 1/2 inch of headspace. Remove any air bubbles, wipe the rims of the jars and lids with a clean cloth and fasten lids.

4. Place into the All American® and process for 15 minutes at a full rolling boil. Turn off flame, remove cover and allow jars to sit in a pot for a few minutes. Remove from canner and place on a dish towel and allow to cool overnight. Store jars in a cool, dark place.

Zucchini Relish

Tangy relish is always so tasty on hot dogs or burgers. This relish is easy to make and is crunchy and not as sweet as cucumber relish. The most time consuming part of making this relish is dicing all the veggies into tiny pieces. All your hard work will pay off once you taste it. Work it into a tuna or potato salad. Recipe makes 5 half-pints.

Ingredients:

- 5 cups zucchini, diced
- ¼ cup green sweet peppers, diced
- ¼ cup pickling salt
- 1 ¾ cup sugar
- ¼ cup water
- 1 tsp. turmeric
- 1 ½ cup onions, diced
- ¼ cup red sweet peppers, diced
- 1 ½ cup vinegar
- 1 tsp. celery seeds
- ½ tsp. mustard seeds

Directions:

1. Combine onions, peppers and zucchini in a large plastic bowl and add salt. Toss to combine and cover with cold water. Put aside for 3 hours. Drain and rinse with water then drain again.
2. Put vinegar, celery seeds, mustard seeds, sugar, ¼ cup water and turmeric in a large pot. Bring to a boil; stir to dissolve sugar and lower heat. Cook for 3 minutes then add zucchini/pepper mixture and cook for 10 minutes, stirring intermittently.

3. Ladle corn relish into prepared jars, leaving 1/2 inch of headspace. Remove any air bubbles, wipe the rims of the jars and lids with a clean cloth and fasten lids.

4. Place into your All American® and process for 10 minutes at full rolling boil, making sure water covers the tops of the jars by 1-2 inches. Turn off the heat, remove cover and allow jars to sit in the pot for a few minutes. Remove from canner and place on a dish towel and allow to cool.

5. Jars should cool for at least 12 hours before checking seals. Properly sealed jars should be stored in a cool, dark place. Place any unsealed jars in the refrigerator.

Chow-Chow

Found in southern and Appalachian culinary cultures, this vegetable relish has been a regional favorite for well over 100 years. Traditionally prepared towards the end of the harvesting season, the vegetables used to make this relish may vary, although the core vegetables typically remain the same. Cabbage, green tomatoes, onion and bell pepper are at the center of most chow-chow variations. Start this recipe the night before you plan to can, so the salted vegetables have plenty of time to sit. Try chow-chow on sausages, ham, hotdogs, hamburgers, beans and even on fishcakes.

Makes: 4 pints.

Ingredients:

- 5 cups coarsely chopped green tomatoes
- 5 cups coarsely chopped cabbage
- 1 1/2 cups finely chopped yellow onion
- 2 cups coarsely chopped bell pepper, try to use contrasting colors
- 1/3 cup kosher or pickling salt
- 2 1/2 cups apple cider vinegar
- 1 cup packed brown sugar
- 1 tbsp. yellow mustard seeds
- 2 fine minced cloves garlic
- 1 tsp. celery seed
- 1/2 tsp. red pepper flakes

Directions:

1. Stir chopped vegetables together in a large bowl. Stir in the salt until well mixed. Cover the bowl and allow to rest for 4 hours or overnight in the refrigerator.

2. Carefully wash and rinse 4 pint jars. Sterilize lids in a small saucepan, leaving the lids in the hot water until ready to close jars. Fill canner with enough water to cover filled pint jars by an inch and bring to a boil. Reduce heat, sterilize jars, then keep pot at a simmer.

3. Use a colander or sieve to drain the vegetables, then rinse them well. Stir together the vinegar, brown sugar, mustard and celery seeds, garlic and pepper flakes in a large pot until well combined. Set the pot over medium-high heat and let it come to a boil. Drop the temperature down to medium-low and let the pot simmer for 5 minutes, stirring occasionally.

4. Stir in the well drained vegetables. Raise heat to medium-high and return the pot to a boil. Lower the temperature to medium-low. Let the pot simmer for another 10 minutes. Use a slotted spoon to carefully fill the pint jars with the hot vegetables. These jars will need to have ¼ inch of head-space.

5. Remembering to leave a head-space of ¼ inch, pour the cooking liquid over the vegetables in the jars. Carefully clean the rims and threads of the jars, then close the jars with the lids and rings. The tops should be on tightly, but not so tight that they are difficult to open.

6. Put the filled pint jars on the rack inside the All American®. If necessary, add enough water to the canner to ensure that the jars are covered by at least 1 inch of water. Set over medium-high heat and bring to a full, rolling boil. Cover the canner and hold at a hard boil for 10 minutes.

7. Take the jars out of the canner and set in a safe place to fully cool. Remember to refrigerate chow-chow after it is opened.

IKRA

Traditional Slavic Ikra falls into two loose categories, those that use carrots as the main ingredient and those that use eggplant. Some varieties use both. This recipe uses carrots, cabbage and parsnips – true peasant food. The name of this traditional relish reflects Slavic humor and culture, sharp wit and appreciation of irony. Ikra is the Russian word for caviar, a luxury the ruling classes enjoyed at the expense of the often heavily taxed lower classes, most of whom made do with what they could raise and preserve, including this delicious relish, known for centuries as the caviar of the common man. This recipe makes about 4 pints.

INGREDIENTS:

1 cup chopped onions

1 cup olive oil

2 ½ cups coarsely chopped carrots

2 cups shredded cabbage

1 cup chopped parsnips

5 green peppers, chopped

1 sweet red pepper, chopped

1 cup chopped celery

2 cups thick tomato pulp

¼ cup sugar

2 tbsp. salt

¼ tsp. black pepper

1/8 tsp. red pepper

DIRECTIONS:

1. Cook onions in the olive oil in a large, heavy pot over low heat. When the onions begin to turn golden, add the carrots, cabbage, parsnips, peppers and celery. Continue cooking over low heat, stirring frequently, until the vegetables are soft and tender. Stir in the tomato pulp, sugar, salt, black pepper and red pepper. Let the pot simmer for another 15 minutes.

2. While the vegetables are cooking, set up the pressure canner. Sterilize 4 pint jars and their lids. After sterilizing, hold the jars and lids in hot water until ready to fill to keep them sterile. Spread a towel out on a part of the counter, a table or a shelf where the jars will be able to sit undisturbed for at least 12 hours.

3. When the vegetables are done, fill the hot jars, leaving 1 inch of headspace. Use a plastic knife or spatula to remove any air pockets. Carefully wipe jar threads and rims clean, put the lids on and tighten the rings. Process in your All American® pressure canner at 10 pounds of pressure for 30 minutes. Adjust for altitude as required.

4. Following the depressurizing, take the jars out of the canner and put them on a towel covered surface to cool. Do not disturb the jars for at least 12 hours. After that, you can check the jars to make sure they sealed properly.

5. Store those with a good seal in a cool, dark place for up to 12 months. If you find a jar that didn't seal well, store it in the refrigerator and use it within a week.

7

CONDIMENTS & SYRUPS

Teriyaki Sauce

This teriyaki sauce is similar to Worcestershire sauce and can be used with fish or meat. You'll enjoy making your own and won't be able to stomach store bought teriyaki after you go down this rabbit hole... Recipe makes 4 half-pints.

Ingredients:

- 2 cups soy sauce
- 1 cup white vinegar
- 2 tbsp. lemon juice
- 2 cups, brown sugar, light
- 2 tbsp. clear jel
- 4 tbsp. ginger, grated

Directions:

1. Combine sugar, ginger, soy sauce, vinegar and lemon juice in a large pot. Heat over a medium flame and bring to a boil then lower heat and cook for 18 minutes.
2. Take 2 tbsp. of sauce and combine with clear jel then add to mixture, whisk and cook for 2 minutes until thick. Remove from flame.
3. Put mixture into prepared jars, leaving 1/4 inch headspace. Remove any air bubbles, wipe the rims of the jars and lids with a clean cloth and fasten lids. Place into canner and process for 15 minutes at full rolling boil.
4. Turn off the flame, remove cover and allow jars to sit in the pot for a few minutes. Remove from canner and place on a dish towel and allow to cool undisturbed.

TOMATO KETCHUP

Yep, ketchup! A great part of what is driving this new interest in home canning is concern about food quality. People worry about GMO foods, food additives, industrial farming fallout, ranging from the antibiotic problem to depleted soils to mass contamination incidents, and more. They see evidence all around them that they are right to be concerned, such as a weight problem epidemic that spans all age groups, rising chronic disease rates, and a sharp uptick in problem food sensitivities, including extreme, life-threatening food allergies. Enjoy a fine tomato ketchup the way it was meant to be – savory, tangy and delicious. When you make your own ketchup, you know there's no high fructose corn syrup or other unhealthy additives. Grow your own tomatoes or buy from a small local farm and there's less worry about chemicals and poisons. After you master the basic recipe, play with the spices, try different vinegars and make this ketchup your own. This recipe makes six 1/2-pint jars.

INGREDIENTS:

4 quarts cored, chopped tomatoes

1 cup chopped onions

1 cup chopped sweet red pepper

1 ½ tsp. celery seed

1 ½ tsp. mustard seed

½ tsp. whole cloves

½ tsp. allspice

½ tsp. peppercorns

1 3-inch piece cinnamon stick, broken into small pieces

1/8 tsp. cayenne pepper

2 tsp. paprika

1 tbsp. salt

½ cup dark brown sugar

1 ½ cups vinegar

DIRECTIONS:

1. Combine the tomatoes, onions and red pepper in a large, heavy stainless steel pot. Over low heat, cook until the tomatoes release their juice, then turn the heat up to medium. Simmer until the vegetables are nice and soft. Remove from heat.
2. Press the vegetable mixture through a sieve to remove skins and seeds. Put the puree back into the pot and bring to a boil over medium-high heat. Stirring often, let boil for 20 minutes.
3. Tie the celery seeds, mustard seeds, whole cloves, peppercorns and cinnamon stick pieces in a doubled piece of cheesecloth or a scrap of natural muslin. Add the spice bag to the pot and continue to boil until the mixture thickens to a ketchup-like consistency.
4. Stir in the allspice, cayenne pepper, paprika, salt, dark brown sugar and vinegar. Continue to boil until the ketchup reaches desired degree of thickness.
5. While the ketchup thickens, set up the All American®. Make sure to fill it with enough water to cover the filled jars by at least an inch or two. Sterilize jars and lids, then keep them in hot, almost simmering, water until ready to use.
6. When the ketchup is thick enough, remove the spice bag. Taste the ketchup and adjust sugar, salt or other seasonings if necessary, then pour hot ketchup into hot jars, leaving ¼ inch of headspace. Wipe jar rims and threads, put tops on and tighten rings.
7. Process jars in the All American® for 10 minutes, beginning the time when the water returns to a boil after the jars are put in the canner. When the processing is complete, carefully remove jars from the canner and set them on a towel to cool undisturbed for at least 12 hours.
8. After the cooling and resting period, check the seals on the jars. Store properly sealed jars in a dark, cool location for up to 12 months. If there is a jar that didn't seal correctly, store it in the refrigerator and use within a few weeks.

Provencal Tomato Sauce

This is a tomato sauce from the southeast of France, its flavor influenced by Provencal culinary traditions. A bit of orange peel, a touch of fennel, a hint of saffron, these are the flavors of Provence, along with olive oil, tomatoes and garlic. With a sauce like this, a good olive oil is essential. This is meant to be a rich sauce, thick and flavorful, the skilled use of spices drawing out subtle flavors that add depth and fullness to those that are a bit bolder. This is a sauce to be savored. Serve it with fresh pasta, rather than the dried.

Makes: 5 pints.

INGREDIENTS:

- 6 lbs. fresh tomatoes
- 1/3 cup olive oil
- 1 cup onions, diced
- ½ tsp. sugar
- 5 cloves garlic, crushed
- 3 1-inch pieces orange peel
- 6 parsley sprigs
- ½ tsp. fennel seed
- ½ tsp. dried basil
- ¼ tsp. ground coriander
- 1 tsp. salt
- ½ tsp. pepper
- ½ tsp. celery salt

Pinch saffron

DIRECTIONS:

1. Dip tomatoes in boiling water for a few seconds so that their skins will slip right off. After the tomatoes are peeled, halve them. Squeeze the seeds and juice gently out of each tomato half. Chop the tomato pulp. It should measure about 8 cups.

2. Heat the olive oil in a large, heavy-bottomed cooking pot over medium-low heat. When it's hot, add the onions and cover the pot. Let the onions cook for 15 minutes, but do not let them brown, adjusting the heat as needed.

3. Stir in the tomatoes, herbs and spices and remaining ingredients. Simmer for 1 ½ hours, covered and stirring often, taking care to scrape the bottom to avoid sticking and scorching.

4. Set up the All American® as a boiling water canner. Wash, rinse and sterilize 5 pint jars and lids. Leave the jars and lids in the hot water until needed.

5. Remove the orange peel from the sauce, then ladle sauce into clean, hot jars, leaving a head-space of ½ inch. Wipe the rims and threads of the jars clean, then top them with lids and tighten the rings.

6. Place jars on rack in the All American® and bring it to a boil. Process the jars for 45 minutes. Carefully remove the jars from the canner and set in a safe place to cool.

Spicy Barbecue Sauce

This is a full-bodied, rich, flavorful barbecue sauce suitable for use with a variety of meats, including chicken, pork, goat and beef. It is the reduction through slow simmering that is the key to the depth and intensity of the flavor this sauce offers. You'll need to watch the pot carefully while it cooks to avoid any sticking or scorching. If your skin is sensitive to the capsaicin in chile peppers, you may want to protect your hands with a light coat of olive oil or a pair of food service type disposable gloves.

Makes: 5 half-pint jars of sauce.

Ingredients:

- 12 lbs. ripe tomatoes
- 3 cups chopped onions
- 2 ¼ cups chopped celery
- 2 ¼ cups chopped red or green sweet peppers
- ½ cup chopped fresh jalapeño chile peppers, seeds removed
- 3 cloves garlic, quartered
- 2 cups vinegar
- 1 ½ cups packed brown sugar
- 3 tbsp. Worcestershire sauce
- 4 tsp. salt
- 4 tsp. dry mustard
- 4 tsp. paprika
- ½ tsp. ground black pepper

DIRECTIONS:

1. Trim cores and stem ends from tomatoes, then cut them into quarters. In a covered heavy-bottomed, 10-quart non-reactive pot over medium-low heat, simmer the tomatoes until they are soft, about 15 minutes.

2. Add the onions, celery, sweet peppers, jalapeño peppers and garlic to the pot, stirring well after each addition. Raise the heat to medium-high and bring the pot to a boil. Drop the temperature back to medium-low and let simmer for 30 minutes, uncovered.

3. Remove from heat and let cool a few minutes. When the tomato mixture is cool enough to work with, put it through a food mill to remove the skin and seeds. There should be about 19 cups of the tomato mixture to return to the pot.

4. Use a ruler to measure how deep the tomatoes are in the pot. Bring the pot to a boil over medium heat, the drop the temperature back to medium-low and leave the pot to simmer, stirring often, for 1 to 1 ¼ hours, or until the tomato mixture has been reduced by half. Use the ruler to confirm the reduction.

5. Add the vinegar, brown sugar, Worcestershire sauce, salt, dry mustard, paprika and black pepper, stirring until well combined. Let the sauce simmer, uncovered, for another hour or until the sauce has thickened as much as you'd like it to.

6. Set up and prepare the All American® as a hot water canner. Wash, rinse and sterilize 5 half-pint jars and their lids. When the sauce is ready, fill the jars, using a ladle to pour the hot sauce into the hot jars. Be sure to leave a head-space of ½ inch. Wipe the rims and thread of the jars, put on the lids and tighten the rings.

7. Place the jars on the canner rack, adding water, if needed, to cover the jars by at least an inch. Bring the All American® to a boil and process the jars for 20 minutes. Take the jars out of the canner and put them in a safe place to cool.

PECAN SYRUP

Ever wondered if you could get the flavor of perfectly flavored praline in your very own jar in your very own pantry? Wonder no more – this recipe gets it just right, and it's wonderfully simple. What could be more delicious? I honestly don't know. This syrup is ideal for pancakes, waffles, French toast, or any other breakfast that's meant to be a proper treat. Needless to say, it's also perfect for dessert, to drizzle over ice cream, pie, or your favorite cookies. There is no happy like pecan-syrup happy!

INGREDIENTS:

- 8 cups of corn syrup
- 2 cups of water
- 1 ½ cup of brown sugar
- 4 cups of pecans, either in pieces or whole and coarsely chopped
- 2 tsp. of pure vanilla extract

DIRECTIONS:

1. Warm up your canning jars and lids in a bath of hot – but not boiling – water.
2. In a large stovetop pot, combine the corn syrup, sugar, and water and simmer at medium heat, stirring continuously, until the sugar is fully dissolved and the mixture is completely blended, then raise heat and boil for one minute.
3. Reduce heat back to a simmer and mix in the vanilla extract and pecans, before bringing to a light boil while stirring continuously for 5 minutes.
4. Place the hot jars on a dishtowel, and fill each with equal portions of the pecan syrup, using a funnel and ladle as needed, leaving a ¼-inch space at the top.

5. Remove the air bubbles from each jar using a plastic knife and wipe around the rims of each of the jars with a damp cloth. Add the sealing rings to the tops of each jar and seal them finger-tight.

6. Place the jars in your All American® and close the lid. Bring to a boil and allow the steam to vent for 10 minutes. After 10 minutes, close the steam vent and process at 5 pounds of pressure for 10 minutes for quart jars and 8 minutes for pint jars.

7. When timer sounds, remove the lid and allow jars to cool for 10 minutes before removing from the canner. Place jars on a table or counter that has been covered with a towel and allow them to cool overnight. When jars are cooled, check to make sure they have sealed properly and store them for up to a year in a cool, dark place.

BLUEBERRY SYRUP

Who says maple syrup is the only kind of syrup your pantry needs? My momma would slap me if she came to visit and caught me without homemade syrup. Clear jel is used as the thickener in this recipe however it pours out great and you can always adjust the amounts used if you prefer a thinner syrup. If you're like me, you'll scoop it out with a spoon and nibble on it by itself. Hah, don't be like me. Just use your fingers.

INGREDIENTS:

1 cup sugar

2 ½ tbsp. clear jel

5 cups blueberries

½ cup water for clear jel and 2 cups for cooking berries

2 tsp. lemon juice

DIRECTIONS:

1. Add blueberries and 2 cups of water to a large cooking pot. Cook for 10 minutes over a medium flame then reduce heat and cook for 20 additional minutes or until berries burst open.
2. Stir to get juices from berries and remove from flame.
3. Set a fine strainer over a container and pour in berries. Leave undisturbed for an hour or more.
4. Pour 2 cups of juice from blueberries and put into a pot along with lemon juice and sugar. Bring mixture to a boil, stirring frequently. Combine Clear jel and water in a bowl and add to mixture, stir and remove from flame.
5. Put mixture into prepared jars, leaving 1/4 inch headspace. Remove any air bubbles, wipe the rims of the jars and lids with a clean cloth

and fasten lids. Place into the All American® and process for 15 minutes at full rolling boil.

6. Turn off flame, remove cover and allow jars to sit in the pot for a few minutes. Remove from canner and place on a dish towel undisturbed and allow to cool.

8

Pickled Vegetables

SWEET PICKLES

Every canner needs a good sweet pickle recipe. Here's mine. Nothing fancy, Enjoy! Recipe makes 2-3 pints.

INGREDIENTS:

¾ cup pickling salt

3 cups sugar

2 tbsp. pickling spices

3 lbs. pickling cucumbers, rinsed and sliced

2 cups vinegar

DIRECTIONS:

1. Slice cucumbers and combine with salt in a plastic container. Put into refrigerator overnight. Remove from fridge and rinse thoroughly. Put aside until needed.
2. Put leftover ingredients into a saucepan and bring to boil, stirring to combine.
3. Pack cucumbers into prepared jars then add the hot liquid, leaving 1/2 inch headspace. Remove any air bubbles, wipe the rims of the jars and lids with a clean cloth and fasten the lids. Place into pressure canner and process for 15 minutes at a rolling boil.
4. When processing is complete remove cover and allow jars to sit in the pot for a few more minutes. Remove from canner and place on a dish towel and allow to cool. Store in a cool, dark place.

FAIRY TALE EGGPLANT PICKLES

These slim fingerling eggplants are perfect for pickling. Because eggplant is so low in acid, this recipe uses 100 percent vinegar as the pickling liquid, not a mixture of vinegar and water. Serve this pickle in salads, mashed with a bit of olive oil and spread on warm pita bread, or on crackers with a creamy, mild sort of cheese. After canning, let rest for a week before opening for the best flavor. This recipe makes 4 pints.

INGREDIENTS:

- 4 lbs. fairy tale eggplants
- 4 tbsp. kosher salt
- 2 lemons, juiced
- 6 cups red wine vinegar
- 1/2 cup roughly chopped fresh basil
- 2 cloves garlic, minced
- 1 tsp. coarsely ground black pepper

DIRECTIONS:

1. Trim ends from eggplants, then cut lengthwise into quarters or sixths, depending on the size of the eggplant. Toss the eggplant pieces with the kosher salt and the lemon juice and set aside for 2 hours.
2. During this time, set up the All American® and sterilize 4 pint-sized jars and their lids. After sterilizing, let the jars and lids stay in hot water until it is time to use them.
3. Pour the eggplant pieces into a colander and rinse under cold running water. Drain well, gently pressing the water from the eggplant without crushing or damaging the pieces.

4. Bring the vinegar to a boil in a large saucepan. Add the eggplant and let the liquid return to a boil. Let the eggplant boil in the vinegar for 2 minutes, then use a slotted spoon to transfer the eggplant to a bowl. Keep vinegar hot.

5. Toss the eggplant with the basil, garlic and pepper, then put it into prepared jars. Pour hot vinegar into the jars, leaving a full 1/2-inch of headspace. Use a butter knife or thin spatula to remove any air bubbles, adding a little more hot vinegar to keep the headspace at ½ inch if need be.

6. Use a damp, lint-free cloth to wipe jar rims and threads. Put lids on and tighten rings. Process in the All American® for 10 minutes. The boiling water should cover the tops of the jars by a depth of at least 1 inch.

7. After the jars have been in the boiling water for 10 minutes, carefully remove them and set them on a towel to cool, undisturbed for at least 12 hours. After the cooling and settling period, you can check the seals.

8. Store well sealed jars in a cool, dark place for up to 12 months. Store those that have not sealed correctly in the refrigerator and use within a month.

Green Tomato Pickles

Make the most of the end of the growing season with these tasty green tomato pickles. Flavored with turmeric, celery and mustard seeds, brown sugar, onions, bell peppers and hot pepper, these pickles can be used on relish trays, sandwiches and salads. If you prefer a pickle that is more spicy than savory, you can increase the hot pepper. Use red peppers, if you can. The color contrast is quite attractive. However, if red peppers are not available or are exorbitantly expensive compared to the green, go ahead and use the green. This recipe makes 5 pints of pickles.

Ingredients:

- 2 quarts green tomatoes, sliced
- 3 tbsp. salt
- 2 cups vinegar
- 2/3 cup firmly packed dark brown sugar
- 1 cup sugar
- 3 tbsp. mustard seed
- ½ tsp. celery seed
- 1 tsp. turmeric
- 3 cups sliced onions
- 2 large red bell peppers, chopped
- 1 hot red or green pepper, chopped

Directions:

1. In a large, stainless steel bowl, combine tomato slices and salt, then let stand for 12 hours.
2. Pour tomatoes into colander and let them drain thoroughly. Set up the All American® and sterilize 5 pint jars and lids. Leave the sterile jars and lids in hot water until ready to fill.

3. In a large heavy saucepan, stir together vinegar, brown sugar, white sugar, mustard seeds, celery seeds and turmeric. Bring to boiling over low heat, add onions and let return to a boil. Boil the onions for 5 minutes, then add the tomatoes and the peppers. Bring the pan to a boil, still over low heat, and boil for another 5 minutes, stirring frequently with a wooden spoon.

4. Use a slotted spoon to put the green tomato mixture into hot, sterile jars. Bring the vinegar-sugar mixture back to boiling, then pour it into the jars, leaving ½ inch of headspace. Wipe the threads and rims of jars with a clean damp cloth, removing any food particles or residue that could prevent a proper seal from forming.

5. Put the lids on the jars, tighten the rings and process in the All American® for 10 minutes, making sure that the jars are at least one inch below the surface of the boiling water.

6. After the jars have boiled for 10 minutes, remove from canner, taking care not to tilt them too much. Set on a towel to cool where they can sit without being disturbed. Let sit for at least 12 hours, then check to see that the jars have sealed correctly.

7. Store those with good seals in a cool, dark place for up to 1 year. Put those with poor seals in the refrigerator and use within a month.

PICKLED FIGS

Serve the fragrant, delicious pickled fig with warm, Mediterranean or Middle Eastern pita bread, soft and creamy goat milk cheese, plump Greek olives and ripe tomato wedges as an appetizer or first course. Put a dish of these pickles on a buffet table near turkey, duck, venison or other game meats. Sweet and savory with a rich tang, these figs complement the whisper of wilderness in the flavor of game meats perfectly. This recipe makes 8 pints.

INGREDIENTS:

- 4 quarts figs, ripe but still firm
- 5 cups sugar
- 2 quarts water
- 3 cups vinegar
- 2 sticks cinnamon
- 1 tbsp. whole allspice
- 1 tbsp. whole cloves

DIRECTIONS:

1. In a heavy stainless steel pot, heat water and 3 cups sugar over medium heat until sugar dissolves. While water is heating, peel figs. When the sugar is dissolved, add the figs to the pot. Lower the temperature to medium-low and gently simmer the figs, stirring occasionally, for 30 minutes. Decrease the temperature to low if necessary to keep the simmering nice and gentle.

2. Add the remaining 2 cups of sugar and the vinegar to the figs. Tie the cinnamon sticks, whole allspice and whole cloves in a square of clean cheesecloth or natural muslin and add to the pot. Continue to simmer gently until the figs are transparent. Cover the pot and refrigerate for 12 to 24 hours.

3. When ready to finish the figs, set up the All American®. Fill with enough water to cover the jars by a depth of at least 1 inch. Sterilize 8 pint jars and their lids. Hold them in just under simmering, not boiling, water until ready to fill.

4. Remove the spice bag from the figs and bring the pot to medium heat. Bring the pot to a boil and let the figs boil for 5 minutes to make sure they are good and hot. Pack the hot figs into hot jars. Bring the brine back to boiling, then pour it over the figs in the jars, leaving 1/2-inch of headspace.

5. With a clean, damp lint-free cloth, carefully clean the threads and rims of the jars. Put the lids on and tighten the rings to secure. Carefully arrange the jars on the All American® 's rack and process for 15 minutes. Timing begins when the water in the canner has returned to boiling.

6. Carefully, without sloshing the liquid around too much, remove jars from canner. Put them on a towel on a counter or table where the jars can cool undisturbed for at least 12 hours. After the cooling off period has passed, check the quality of the seal on each jar.

7. Those that have sealed correctly can be stored for up to 12 months in a cool, dark place. Those that didn't seal as well as they should have can be stored in the refrigerator. Use these within 1 month.

Cowboy Candy (Sweet Pickled Jalapeños)

Howdy partners! These sweet jalapeños are crunchy, spicy and sweet and go great with burgers or hot dogs. Let your jalapeños soak at least a week in the jar to get the true burst of flavors from your peppers. You can use any variety of jalapeños that you prefer or are able to find out on the range. This recipe will have you hanging up your spurs to sit and munch for a spell. Recipe makes 2 pints.

Ingredients:

- 1 cup of Jalapeño peppers
- 2 cups of raw cane sugar
- ½ tsp. of ground turmeric
- 2 to 3 tsp. of garlic powder
- ¾ cup of cider vinegar
- 1 ½ tbsp. mustard seeds
- ½ tsp. of cayenne pepper
- ½ tsp. of celery seed

Directions:

1. Slice the jalapeño peppers, place in a bowl and set aside. In a saucepan over medium heat, add the sugar, celery seed, cayenne, vinegar, turmeric, garlic powder, and mustard seed and bring to a boil. Reduce to low heat and add the sliced jalapeño, cook for 5 more minutes and remove from heat.

2. Pack peppers into prepared jars then add liquid, leaving 1/4 inch of headspace. Remove any air bubbles, wipe the rims of the jars and lids with a clean cloth and fasten lids. Place into the prepared All American® pressure canner and process for 15 minutes at full rolling boil.

3. Remove from heat and allow jars to sit in the pot for a few minutes. Remove from canner and place on a dish towel undisturbed and allow to cool completely.
4. If jars make a popping sound that means they are cooling and sealing. Check seals and reseal any unsealed jar. Store until needed.

Pickled Baby Artichokes

Use freshly picked artichokes and pickle them the same day. Larger artichokes require trimming and other preparation before canning. This brine can be used to can mushrooms and peppers also. Recipe makes 4-5 pints.

Ingredients:

- 1 cup lemon juice
- 1 cup extra virgin olive oil
- 2 cups white vinegar
- 40 Artichokes, small

Directions:

1. Prepare canning equipment. Set up the water canning equipment or a pot large enough to hold jars, sterilize jars and lids, and keep them in hot water until ready to use.
2. Combine all ingredients except artichokes in a sauce pan and heat to just below simmering. Rinse and clean artichokes.
3. Pack artichokes into prepared jars then add the hot liquid, leaving 1/2 inch of headspace. Remove any air bubbles, wipe the rims of the jars and lids with a clean cloth and fasten lids.
4. Place into the All American® and process for 30 minutes at full rolling boil. Turn off flame, remove cover and allow jars to sit in the pot for a few minutes. Remove from canner and place on a dish towel and allow to cool overnight.

SPICED PICKLED BEETS

Beets can be used in a variety of ways but they are widely used in juices. You can add these beets to your salads or prepare them as a side dish. Beets aid in lowering blood pressure and can help boost one's stamina. They actually increase your lung capacity so they are a staple for endurance athletes. I gobbled them up constantly back in my running days. Now I'm more into the gobbling and less into the running. If you're not comfortable with all of the spices I use, just adapt it to your taste. Recipe makes 4 pints.

INGREDIENTS:

- 8-15 Beets
- 2 cups white vinegar
- 16 whole cloves
- 2 tsp. pickling salt
- 2 cups sugar
- 1/3 cup water
- 8 whole allspice berries
- 2 cinnamon sticks
- 1 tbsp. olive oil
- Salt
- Pepper
- 1 tbsp. Garlic, diced

DIRECTIONS:

1. Set oven to 375°F. Scrub beets and place into a baking dish. Use olive oil to drizzle all over the beets then add pepper, salt and garlic. Toss and roast for 30 minutes, until tender.

2. Remove from oven, cool and peel skin. Cut into rounds. Put water, vinegar and sugar in a saucepan and heat until it comes to a boil, stir frequently. Keep hot over a low flame until needed.

3. Put 2 allspice berries, ½ tsp. salt, 4 cloves and ½ cinnamon stick into each jar. Pack beets into prepared jars then add hot liquid, leaving 1/2 inch of headspace.

4. Remove any air bubbles, wipe the rims of the jars and lids with a clean cloth and fasten lids. Place into the All American® and process for 30 minutes at full rolling boil.

5. Turn off flame, remove cover and allow jars to sit in the pot for a few minutes.

6. Remove from canner and place on a dish towel and allow to cool undisturbed.

7. If jars make a popping sound that means they are cooling and sealing. Check seals and reseal any unsealed jar. Store until needed.

SANDRA MAY

9

CANNED VEGETABLES

HOME CANNED SOUP VEGETABLES

Use your own fresh garden vegetables, pick some up at a nearby farmers' market, or buy some from your local organic farmer and you can have convenience you can trust. With a jar of these vegetables, you're halfway to a pot of soup when a chilly evening marks the end of a hectic day. A jar of vegetables, a few pantry ingredients and a little something from the refrigerator or freezer can make a nourishing, appetizing dinner quick and easy to put together during the workweek. When you make your own convenience foods, you don't have to worry about factory farm chemicals and other food industry threats. When canning mixed vegetables or other items with mixed ingredients, the processing time will be the amount of time that the ingredient with the longest processing time requires for safe canning. This recipe makes about 8 pints.

INGREDIENTS:

- 1 ¾ lbs. carrots, in 1/3-inch thick slices
- ¾ lb. green beans, cut into 2 inch pieces
- 1 lb. small onions, quartered
- 1 lb. celery, sliced
- 2 tbsp. salt
- 1 tbsp. pepper
- 1 ½ quarts chicken stock or hot water
- ¼ cup fresh parsley, minced

DIRECTIONS:

1. Fill your All American® with water to 3 or 4 inches deep. Once the water is in, start getting it hot. Wash, rinse and sterilize 8 pint jars and lids.
2. Using a large pot, add the vegetables, salt and pepper and cover with water. Bring the pot to a boil, then lower the heat slightly. Let the pot

simmer for about 5 minutes. In a large saucepan, bring the chicken broth to a boil.

3. Pack each sterile jar with the hot vegetables, then pour the hot broth over the vegetables. Fill each jar to 1 inch below the jar's rim, so that there will be one full inch of head-space under the lid. Use a thin plastic knife to break up any air bubbles, then divide the fresh parsley evenly between the jars. With a clean, damp cloth carefully wipe the rim and threads of each jar, then put the lids on and tighten the rings as securely as you can.

4. Add jars to the pressure canner. Close the lid and processed at 10 pounds of pressure for 30 minutes. After the processing time is completed, let gauge return to zero. Remove lid from the pressure canner and let jars sit for 10 minutes before removing. Place jars on a clean towel and let them sit overnight undisturbed.

5. After 24 hours, check all seals. Jars with good seals can be stored in a cool, dark place for up to 1 year. Those that did not seal properly should be refrigerated and used within 3 days.

Roast Tomatoes

Choose firm, fresh tomatoes when you are picking your tomatoes to can. The best types of tomatoes to use for canning are Roma, Beefsteak, Lemon Boy and Better Boy. These are not very thick and cook much faster than other varieties. Your canned roasted tomatoes can be stored in a cool dark place for up to 12 months. Recipe should make about 9 pints.

Ingredients:

- 13 lbs. of ripe red fresh tomatoes
- 1-2 tbsp. of mixed Italian herbs
- 9 tbsp. of fresh lemon juice
- 4 1/2 tsp. of salt

Directions:

1. Set oven to 450°F. Wash tomatoes and slice into half and place cut sides onto roasting pan. Add herbs if desired and roast until tomatoes are wrinkled and tender, usually about 1 hour.
2. Add one tbsp. of lemon juice to each prepared jar then add in the roasted tomatoes, press into jars leaving 1 inch headspace. Add ½ tsp. of salt in each jar if desired. Wipe the rims of the jars and lids. Close jars as tightly as possible and place them into the prepared pressure canner. Close the lid and process with a pressure of 10-10 pounds for 25 minutes.
3. Lower the temperature and let gauge return to zero. Remove lid from pressure canner and let jars sit for 10 minutes inside before removing. Place on a towel in a safe place to cool overnight before checking the seals and storing properly.

SLICED GREEN TOMATOES

I love the tartness of green tomatoes. Pick some tomatoes before they turn red or buy em green and prepare these tomatoes that can be fried later. These will definitely come in handy whenever you need a batch of fried tomatoes (for me that is often). The simple brine preserves the natural goodness of the tomatoes until needed.

INGREDIENTS:

- 2 tbsp. of fresh lemon juice
- 8 cups of fresh green tomatoes
- 1 tsp. of salt
- Water, as needed to cover the tomatoes

DIRECTIONS:

1. Remove the cores of the tomatoes, cut off the tops. Slice them into ¼ inch thick rounds. Add water in a large pot, about 5 to 6 cups, and heat until it starts to bubble. Do not bring to a boil.
2. Pack tomatoes on top of each other in the prepared jars, and then add 1 tbsp. of lemon juice and ½ tsp. of salt to each jar.
3. Then pour in with warm water, leaving 1/2 inch headspace. Remove any air bubbles, wipe the rims of the jars and lids with a clean cloth and fasten the lids.
4. Place into the All American® pressure canner and close the lid. Process the tomatoes for 35 minutes at full rolling boil. Turn off the flame, remove cover and allow jars to sit in the pot for a few minutes. Remove from canner and place on a dish towel and allow to cool at least 12 hours.

MARINATED MUSHROOMS

These mushrooms will beat any canned mushroom you will ever buy. Use whatever mushrooms you prefer to make this recipe, just be sure they are very fresh. Add your mushrooms to any soup, pasta or salad. No more store bought mushrooms after you taste this. Recipe makes 9 half-pints.

INGREDIENTS:

- 6 lbs. of small whole mushrooms
- 2 cups of olive oil
- 2 to 3 tsp. of dried oregano leaves
- 1 tbsp. pickling salt
- 3 to 4 tbsp. of minced pimiento
- 1 tbsp. of whole black peppercorns
- ½ cup of freshly squeezed organic lemon juice
- 2 to 2 ½ cups of white vinegar
- 2 to 3 tsp. of dried basil leaves
- ½ cup of diced white onion
- 2 to 3 garlic cloves, sliced into 4 portions

DIRECTIONS:

1. Put mushrooms and lemon juice in a large pot over medium-high heat, and pour in just enough water to cover. Cover pot and bring to a boil, cook for 5 minutes. Remove from heat and drain.
2. Combine together the vinegar, basil, oregano, oil, salt and basil in a saucepan. Add pimiento and onions, stir to combine and apply medium-high heat. Heat the mixture until it starts to boil. Remove saucepan from heat and set aside.

3. Put 2 to 3 whole peppercorns and a slice of garlic into each prepared jar. Add the mushrooms into the jars and pour in the seasoned olive oil mixture, leaving ½ inch of headspace. Remove any air bubbles, wipe the rims of the jars and lids with a clean cloth and fasten the lids.

4. Place into the All American® pressure canner, close the lid and process for 20 minutes at a full rolling boil. Make sure water covers the jars by 1-2 inches.

5. Turn off the heat, remove cover and allow jars to sit in the pot for a few minutes. Remove from canner and place on a dish towel undisturbed and allow to cool.

Glazed Carrots

Tom Colicchio, the celebrity chef judge on the TV show, Top Chef, forever changed the way I think about carrots with one of his recipes for a simple side dish of honey glazed carrots. Carrots when glazed become candy. These glazed carrots with brown sugar are great for the kids especially if they don't enjoy eating carrots as is. You'll love em too.

Ingredients:

- 2 cups brown sugar
- 1 cup orange juice
- 7 lbs. carrots
- 2 cups water

Directions:

1. Wash and peel carrots; rinse again and slice carrots into 3 pieces. Slice the thick ends of carrots lengthwise down the middle.
2. Combine water, orange juice and brown sugar in a saucepan and cook until mixture get syrupy. Cover to keep hot and turn off the flame.
3. Put carrots into jars, packing them a closely as possible. Fill jars with hot syrup and leave 1" headspace. Wipe the rims and lids of the jars with a clean towel.
4. Close jars as tightly as possible. Close lid and bring to a boil then allow steam to vent for 10 minutes. Close vent and pressure at 10 lbs for 30 minutes.
5. Allow jars to cool for 10 minutes before removing and placing them on a towel in a safe space. Allow them to cool overnight before checking seals and properly storing in a cool, dark place.

GREEN BEANS

Fresh green beans can be an excellent side dish to many meals. Both healthy and tasty, green beans usually grow in abundance in the summer garden. Now you can preserve them for those winter months when the only green beans you and in stores are small and wilted. To avoid the beans being too soft when canned, raw pack them. Recipe makes 7 quarts

INGREDIENTS:

14 lbs. green beans

7 tsp salt

Water, as needed

DIRECTIONS:

1. Wash the beans, remove the stems but leave tip of beans. Snap beans to desired length. one to two inches is sufficient, but you may leave them longer if desired
2. Place the beans into the sterilized jars. Add boiling water to cover the beans leaving 1/2 inch of headspace. Make sure to remove all air bubbles. Add salt if desired and wipe the rims and lids of the jars.
3. Close jars as tightly as possible and place them into the prepared pressure canner. Close the lid and pressure them at 10 pounds for 25 minutes or 20 minutes if using pints.
4. Once the pressure canner has been depressurized and vented, remove jars from the canner and put them on a towel on the counter to cool. Let the jars sit for at least 12 hours without being disturbed. Then, check all seals. Store safely sealed jars for up to 1 year in a cool, dark place.

HERBED PEAS

Peas are great and healthy but when they're plain, well, they're just plain. Thyme and chervil add to the flavor of the peas so that you don't just have to feed them to infants. With a little flavor, you'll enjoy them. Recipe makes 1-2 pints.

INGREDIENTS:

- 1 tsp. of dried thyme leaves
- 6 cups of Peas
- Water, as needed to cover the peas
- 1 tsp. of Chervil

DIRECTIONS:

1. Sort and wash peas and drain. Place the peas into a pot and pour with water just enough to cover the peas. Apply medium-high heat and bring to a boil. Cook for 5 minutes and remove the pot from heat. Let it stand for 1 hour and then drain, reserving half of the cooking liquid.

2. Put prepared jars on a clean dish towel. Fill the jars with peas and add ½ tsp. of chervil and ½ tsp. of thyme to each jar. Bring reserved liquid to a boil and add to the jars. Make sure to cover the peas while leaving 1 inch of headspace and no air bubbles in the jar. Wipe the rims and lids of the jars with a cloth and close the lids tightly.

3. Place the jars into the prepared pressure canner and close the lid. Bring to a boil and let it steam for 10 minutes with open steam vent. Close the vent and process with a pressure of 10 pounds for 40 minutes.

4. When canner has reached zero pressure, cool jars for approximately 10 minutes before removing from the canner. Place jars on a towel in a safe space to cool completely. Check seals after at least 12 hours. Jars that have sealed properly can be stored in a cool, dark place for

12 months. Jars that did not seal properly should be placed in the refrigerator and used within 3-5 days.

CORN

Store bought canned corn is filled with sweeteners, salt and preservatives. Isn't everything at the store? Corn is not only tasty but has many benefits such as lowering hypertension and controlling diabetes. This canned corn is simply fresh, plain ole corn and water. Sugar and salt could be added. Recipe makes 4 pints.

INGREDIENTS:

4 cups hot water

10 ears white corn

DIRECTIONS:

1. Husk the corn, take out silk and rinse. Remove corn from the cob by cutting. Put water in a pot and boil.
2. Put corns into jars, fill jars with hot water and leave 1" headspace. Wipe the rims and lids of the jars with a clean towel.
3. Close jars as tightly as possible. Close lid and bring to a boil then allow steam to vent for 10 minutes. Close vent and pressure at 10 lbs for 55 minutes.
4. Once the pressure canner has been depressurized and vented, remove jars and set them on a towel to cool. Let them sit, undisturbed, for at least 12 hours, then check seals. Put correctly sealed jars in a cool, dark place for up to 12 months.

Mexican Style Corn

Mexican food is often spicy and rich in flavor. By adding a few spices and peppers to these corns, a Mexican essence is added. This corn only gets better with time as it marinates in the spices. You may add salt or sugar for added flavor. Recipe makes 2 pints.

Ingredients:

- 2 tsp. red onion, chopped
- 2 tsp. red bell peppers
- 2 ½ cups Corn
- 2 tsp. jalapeno peppers
- 1 tsp. Cilantro, minced

Directions:

1. Remove corn from the cob and put into a bowl. Mix with other ingredients. Put mixture into jars and fill jars with hot water and leave 1" headspace. Wipe the rims and lids of the jars with a clean towel. Remove air spaces with a spoon or spatula.
2. Close lid and bring to a boil then allow steam to vent for 10 minutes. Close vent and pressure at 10 lbs for 55 minutes.
3. When the canner has depressurized, allow jars to cool for 10 minutes before removing and placing them on a towel in a safe space. Allow them to cool overnight before checking seals and properly storing in a cool, dark place.

Chard, Collards, and Kale

This is a simple and efficient way to keep a serving of greens on hand when needed. Green leafy vegetables play a keen role in maintaining one's health as they contain many properties that can help your well-being. They aid in lowering cholesterol, maintaining good eye sight and preventing cancer. Plus, they're really tasty! Use only fresh vegetables when canning. Recipe makes 9 pints.

Ingredients:

- 6 lbs. chard
- 6 lbs. kale
- 6 lbs. collards

Directions:

1. Wash greens one at a time and drain. Remove stems and ribs from the middle. Put 1 lb of mixed greens into a cheesecloth bag and steam until wilted (for about 5 minutes). Repeat until all greens are blanched.

2. Put blanched greens into jars with fresh boiling water and a pinch of salt if so desired. Make sure to leave 1" head space. Make sure there are no air bubbles. Wipe the rims and lids of the jars with a clean towel.

3. Close jars as tightly as possible. Close pressure canner lid and bring to a boil then allow steam to vent for 10 minutes. Close vent and pressure at 10 lbs for 70 minutes. If you are using quart sized jars pressure for 90 minutes. Let gauge return to zero. Remove lid from pressure canner and let jars sit for 10 minutes inside before removing. Place jars on a clean towel and let them sit until cool.

Garlic Dill Zucchini

Zucchini plants often are among the star producers in the home garden. Indeed, zucchini plants can be overwhelmingly prolific. At the height of the season, it can be difficult to give it away. Of course, canners never have such problems. They know exactly what to do with an abundance of produce. This recipe produces a delicious dill and garlic infused zucchini. During your garden's peak zucchini production period, it can be hard to imagine ever craving some of this summer vegetable again. However, after the harvest season is done and a couple months have gone by, you'll be glad to see these jars on your pantry shelf. This recipe makes 5 to 6 pints.

Ingredients:

6 lbs. zucchini, unpeeled, sliced thin

2 cups celery, sliced thin

2 large onions, chopped

1/3 cup salt

½ cup white sugar

2 tbsp. dill weed

2 cups white vinegar

3 cloves garlic

Directions:

1. Put the zucchini, celery and onions in a large glass or stainless steel bowl. Sprinkle with salt and toss to combine. Cover vegetables with ice cubes and let sit for 3 hours. After three hours, rinse and drain the vegetables well. Set aside.
2. While waiting for the vegetables to be ready, set up the All American® pressure canner and sterilize the jars and lids. Leave them in steady simmering water until needed.

3. Combine the sugar, dill weed and vinegar in a large stainless steel pot and apply high heat. Bring the pot to a boil while stirring constantly. Stir in the drained vegetables, and cook until it returns to a boil. Remove pot from heat and set aside.

4. Fill the sterilized jars with the warm vegetables and liquid, leaving ½ inch of headspace. Drop ½ clove of garlic in each jar, wipe the jar rims and threads with a clean damp cloth and close with hot lids. Tighten rings and put the jars in the All American®.

5. Process the jars for 10 minutes after the water has returned to a boil. After time is complete, carefully remove jars to a towel covered counter to cool. Let sit for at least 12 hours, before checking to see if the jars sealed properly.

Sweet Potatoes

I'm a big fan of sweet potatoes. They're cheap, they're potatoes, they're sweet, and you can cook them a thousand ways. This recipe is easy to prepare and can be had alone or with meat/ vegetables. Use this for a pie filling, casserole, or any of the 998 other ways. This recipe is the general way I can sweet potatoes which can later on be used and flavored however you like. Recipe makes 1 quart.

Ingredients:

- ½ cup brown sugar
- 2 lbs. of sweet potatoes
- 1 cup water
- ¼ tsp. of cinnamon

Directions:

1. Wash potatoes and add into a pot with boiling water. Boil for 15 minutes with skin on. Drain the potatoes and remove the skin. Cut the potatoes into cubes.
2. While boiling the potatoes, combine the water, cinnamon and sugar in a pan over high heat. Cook until it starts to thicken and caramelize while stirring regularly.
3. Put prepared jars on a clean dish towel. Fill jars with potatoes and pour in the syrup, leaving 1 inch headspace. Make sure there are no air bubbles and wipe the rims and lids of the jars clean. Cover the jars tightly and place into the prepared pressure canner.
4. Close pressure canner lid, bring to a boil then let it steam for 10 minutes with open steam vent. Close the vent and process with a pressure of 10 pounds for 90 minutes, or 75 minutes if using pint jars.
5. When canner has depressurized, allow jars to sit undisturbed for 10 minutes before removing. Remove and place jars on a towel in a safe spot to cool overnight.

CANDIED YAMS

Is there really a Sasquatch? How exactly did those pyramids get built? What's the difference between a sweet potato and a yam? These questions have long been pondered and debated. Think I'm kidding? Okay I yam. I know, I know, I can't help it sometimes. For most folks, sweet potatoes and yams are interchangeable, as what most of us call yams, are really just sweet potatoes. Here's the good news. Either of them combined with brown sugar and canned…are fabulous. Candied yams are a Thanksgiving tradition. Canning your yams long before Thanksgiving will ensure that your yams get more time to marinate in cinnamon and other spices. I used "your yams" twice in that sentence! Candied yams can last up to a year and will have everyone talking about your yams. Recipe makes 6 pints.

INGREDIENTS:

- 2 cups brown sugar
- 1 cup sugar
- 1 tsp. vanilla
- 1 tsp. nutmeg
- 12 yams
- 2 cups orange juice
- 1 cup water
- 2 tsp. cinnamon
- ¼ cup lemon juice

DIRECTIONS:

1. Peel yams and cut into chunks. Heat water and put in yams. Let it sit for 5 minutes then drain water from yams; try not to mash them. Mix all other ingredients in a large saucepan and bring to a boil. Gently fold in the yams, being careful that they don't become mashed.

2. Put prepared jars on a clean dish towel. Fill jars with yam then add in syrup; be sure to leave 1 inch headspace. A bit of water may be added to the syrup in order to have plenty to fill all the jars. Make sure there are no air bubbles. Wipe the rims and lids of the jars.
3. Add jars to the pressure canner, close the lid and bring to a boil. Allow steam to vent for 10 minutes. Close vent and pressure at 10 lbs for 90 minutes or 75 minutes if using pint jars. Once the pressure canner has been depressurized and vented, remove jars from the canner and put them on a towel on the counter to cool. Let the jars sit for at least 12 hours without being disturbed. Then, check all seals. Store safely sealed jars for up to 1 year in a cool, dark place.

SANDRA MAY

10

Juices & Fruits

STRAWBERRY PINEAPPLE LEMONADE CONCENTRATE

Strawberries blend with lemon and pineapple for a fresh tropical blend. The sugar can easily be replaced with another desired sweetener that is safe for canning. Use very ripe fruits so that you can use as little sugar as possible, but if you sugar fiends wish to increase the sugar, you are free to do so. Recipe makes 6-8 pints.

INGREDIENTS:

- 3 cups fresh pineapple
- 4 cups sugar
- 3 cups strawberries
- 4 cups freshly squeezed lemon juice

DIRECTIONS:

1. Puree pineapple and strawberries using a food processor or blender. Put puree in a large pot. Heat mixture but do not boil. Add sugar and lemon juice and stir. Use a thermometer to test temperature of mixture. Remove from heat when it gets to 190°F.

2. Ladle hot mixture into prepared jars, leaving 1/4 inch of headspace. Remove any air bubbles, wipe the rims of the jars and lids with a clean cloth and fasten lids.

3. Place into your All American® and process for 10 minutes at full rolling boil. Turn off heat, remove cover and allow jars to sit in the pot for a few minutes. Remove from canner and place on a dish towel undisturbed and allow to cool overnight.

4. **Add one part water to one part concentrate when mixing.

PINA COLADA CONCENTRATE

I'll never forget wandering into Braselito, Costa Rica on my honeymoon after I was careless and left our doors unlocked and got my new wife's wallet stolen. We had been in the country for about a half hour! But we found the nearest bar and Pina Coladas made everything seem okay and worrying about how to get her back into the U.S. could wait for another day. I don't often drink Pina Coladas, but when I do...I think about Costa Rica and smile. We cannot safely can coconut cream so we have replaced it with coconut extract. Just add rum or other desired liquid to this concentrate when you use. Recipe makes 6-8 pints.

INGREDIENTS:

- 6 cups fresh pineapple
- 6 cups of sugar
- 1 tbsp. coconut extract
- 4 cups of fresh organic lemon juice

DIRECTIONS:

1. Puree the pineapple into a coarse mixture using a food processor or blender. Transfer the puree to large pot, turn on medium heat and cook until it starts to simmer. Do not boil. Add sugar, coconut extract and lemon juice in the pot and cook until it reaches 190°F, while stirring regularly. Use a thermometer to test temperature of mixture. Remove pot from heat.
2. Ladle the hot mixture into the prepared jars, leaving 1/4 inch headspace. Remove any air bubbles and wipe the rims of the jars and the lids with a clean cloth, fasten lids.
3. Place into your prepared All American® pressure canner and process for 15 minutes at full rolling boil.

4. Turn off heat source, remove cover and allow jars to sit in the pot for a few more minutes. Remove from canner and place on a dish towel and allow them to cool undisturbed.

Fruit Salad

I love canning fruit and often will toss all kinds right in together. Fruit salads can consist of whatever fruits you prefer and in any proportion you like. Canning your own fruit salads can ensure that you put exactly what you want into each serving. It can serve as a way to preserve many seasonal fruits. The sweetness of the simple syrup can also be altered to your liking.

Ingredients:

- 1 chopped pineapple
- 2 lbs. apricots, peeled and diced
- 2 lbs. apples, peeled and diced
- 2 lbs. seedless grapes
- 2 cups pineapple juice, unsweetened
- 5 cups sugar
- 2 lbs. peaches, peeled and chopped
- 2 lbs. plums, minced
- 2 lbs pears, peeled and diced
- 2 lbs. Bing cherries, pitted and halved
- 8 cups water
- 2-3 cups lemon juice to keep fruit from browning

Directions:

1. Peel fruits that need to have their skins removed, remove cores and pits of fruits and cover them with lemon juice. Toss gently and put aside until needed.

2. Put water and sugar in a saucepan and bring to a boil. Drain lemon juice from fruits.

3. Ladle ½ cup of hot sugar water into prepared jars. Add fruit and a little more syrup if necessary; be sure to leave 1/2 inch of headspace. Remove any air bubbles, wipe the rims of the jars and lids with a clean cloth and fasten lids.

4. Place into the All American® and process for 20 minutes at a full rolling boil. Turn off flame, remove cover and allow jars to sit in the pot for a few more minutes. Remove from canner and place on a dish towel undisturbed and allow to cool.

Honey Blood Orange Slices

This is my second blood orange recipe in this book. They're just that amazing. Adding simple ingredients emphasizes this orange's unique flavor. The syrup yielded from this recipe can be used in cocktails if you're into that sort of thing.

Ingredients:

1 tbsp. of whole cloves

Water, as needed

2 ½ cups of honey

5 to 6 cinnamon sticks

5 lbs. of blood oranges, sliced into wedges or rounds

1/3 cup of fresh organic lemon juice

2 ½ cups sugar

Directions:

1. Put oranges in a large non-reactive pot and pour in water just to cover the oranges. Apply medium heat, bring to a boil and cook for 15 minutes or until the skin is tender. Remove the pot from heat and set aside.

2. Add sugar, lemon juice and honey in another pot, apply medium-high heat and cook until the sugar is completely dissolved, stirring frequently. Add 1 ½ cups of cooking liquid from oranges and add in the cloves and cinnamon. Using a slotted spoon remove the oranges from the pot and transfer into the sugar-lemon mixture. Boil for 40 minutes until oranges are glazed all over while stirring occasionally.

3. Remove from flame and use a slotted spoon to pack orange slices into prepared jars, leaving 1 inch headspace or slightly more.

4. Top with syrup and remove any air bubbles. Wipe the rims of the jars and lids with a clean cloth and fasten lids.

5. Place into the prepared All American® pressure canner and process for 10 minutes at full rolling boil. When finished, remove jars from the canner. Place on a towel on a counter to cool overnight. Check seals and store in a cool, dark place.

CANDIED KUMQUATS

Kumquats are from the citrus family but are as small as olives. They can be used in making jelly or marmalade and can even be used as a garnish for cocktails (not that I would know anything about cocktails). Candied kumquats can be used in preparing cakes and other desserts. Taking the seeds out may be time consuming but this rare fruit is worth the trouble. Recipe makes 2 pints.

INGREDIENTS:

- 2 cups sugar
- 2/3 cup water
- 4 cups free Kumquats

DIRECTIONS:

1. Remove seeds from kumquats and make an "X" in each fruit. Put into water (cold) and put aside.
2. Combine water and sugar in a saucepan and cook for 2 minutes, stirring frequently. Drain fruits and add to sugar mixture and cook for 10 minutes. Be sure to stir to avoid burning. Remove from heat.
3. Ladle hot kumquats and syrup into prepared jars, leaving 1/2 inch headspace. Remove any air bubbles, wipe the rims of the jars and lids with a clean cloth and fasten lids.
4. Place into your All American® and process for 10 minutes at a full rolling boil. Water should cover the jars by an inch or two.
5. When complete, turn off the heat, remove cover and allow jars to sit in the pot for a few minutes. Remove from canner and place on a dish towel and allow to cool.

Maraschino Cherries

Small, sour Mascara cherries are usually used to make maraschino cherries however these are grown in Italy and South Hungary. You would have to import these cherries if you specifically want to use those. This recipe uses a great replacement of either Bing or Rainer's cherries. The difference will simply be in the color of the cherries after they are soaked in brine. This recipe takes at least 2 days to complete, but it's worth it! Recipe makes 2-3 pints.

Ingredients:

- 4 ½ lbs. pitted red cherries
- 3 cups water
- 2 tbsp. almond extracts
- 8 cups sugar
- 1 squeezed lemon
- 2 tbsp. red food coloring

For brine:

- 8 cups water
- 2 tbsp. Pickling salt

Directions:

1. Heat brine ingredients and add pitted cherries. Soak overnight, drain and rinse.
2. Combine 3 cups of water, lemon juice, cherries, coloring and sugar in a large pot. Bring to a boil, remove from heat and let it sit for a day. Remove cherries from liquid and heat liquid; return cherries to pot and let it sit for another 24 hours. Take cherries from liquid again, reheat liquid, add almond extract and return cherries to the pot.

3. Pack cherries into prepared jars using a slotted spoon then add liquid, leaving 1 inch of headspace. Remove any air bubbles, wipe the rims of the jars and lids with a clean cloth and fasten lids.

4. Place into the All American® and process for 20 minutes at full rolling boil. Turn off flame, remove canner cover and allow jars to sit in the pot for a few minutes. Remove from canner and place on a dish towel and allow to cool undisturbed.

SPICED PEARS

These pears are cold packed, sometimes called raw packed, so they are not cooked before they go into the jars. When using the cold pack method, jars are typically filled a bit fuller, or packed tighter, than they are when using the hot pack method. That is because the food is expected to shrink some during processing and cooling. To prevent the pared pears from discoloring while waiting for the syrup to boil, put them in a bowl with enough water to cover them, then stir in the juice of a lemon or two. Drain them just before using.

Makes: 3 - 4 quarts, depending on how tight the jars are packed.

INGREDIENTS:

12 to 14 cups pears, peeled, cut in half, and cored

10 cups water

Juice of one lemon

2 to 3 cups sugar

1 stick cinnamon per jar

1 dime sized piece of ginger root per jar

3 whole cloves per jar

7 whole peppercorns per jar

1 cardamom pod per jar

DIRECTIONS:

1. Prepare canning equipment. Fill the All American® with enough water to cover the filled jars by at least an inch. Bring the canner to a boil, then reduce heat to low and keep it at a simmer. Wash, rinse and sterilize jars and lids, leaving them in simmering water until needed.

2. Stir the water, lemon juice and sugar together in a large pot over medium heat, stirring until the sugar dissolves. Continue cooking over medium heat, stirring occasionally, until the syrup comes to a boil.

3. While waiting for the syrup to boil, prepare hot, sterilized jars for the syrup. For each jar, fill to the halfway point with pears, drop the spices in, then fill the rest of the way with more pears, leaving ½ inch of head-space at the top.

4. Use a ladle to pour the hot syrup over the pears, filling each jar until you reach the ½ inch needed for head-space. Wipe the rims and threads of the jars, making sure that there is no syrup residue remaining, as that can interfere with the proper sealing of a jar. After the rims and threads are clean, put on the lids and tighten the rings.

5. Put the filled, closed jars on the canner rack. The water in the All American® should cover the jars by at least 1 inch. Add more water if necessary. Bring the water in the canner to a boil. Keep the water at a boil and process the jars for 30 minutes.

6. Carefully take the jars out of the canner and set them on a towel to cool. After 24 hours, check the seal on each jar. These pears can be stored in a dark, cool place for up to 12 months.

Port and Cinnamon Plums

These delicious plums can be served in a variety of ways. They make a nice dessert or snack just as they are. However, you can also pour them into a saucepan, take out the cinnamon stick and orange peel, then simmer over medium heat to reduce the syrup. After the syrup is reduced to your liking, you can spoon the warm plums and reduced syrup over pound cake, short cake, or something similar, perhaps topped with a bit of whipped cream or a scoop of premium vanilla ice cream. These plums aren't just for dessert. You can also serve them alongside of beef that has been slow-cooked or roasted, allowing the rich flavors of each to complement the other.

Makes: 7 pints.

Ingredients:

- 4 lbs. plums
- 1 orange
- 4 cups water
- 2 1/3 cups sugar
- ¾ cup ruby port
- ¼ tsp. salt
- 7 3-inch cinnamon sticks

Directions:

1. Cut plums into quarters and remove pits, then set them aside and prepare canning equipment. Fill the boiling water canner with enough water to cover filled and capped jars by at least an inch. Bring the water to a boil, then lower the heat and keep it at a simmer. Carefully wash, rinse and sterilize 7 pint jars and their lids. Keep the jars and lids in simmering water until it's time to use them.

2. With a vegetable peeler, remove the peel from the orange in strips between 2 and 3 inches long, using a sharp paring knife to trim away the white parts. Squeeze the orange over a measuring cup until there is 1/3 cup juice. Pour the juice into a large, heavy-bottomed saucepan. Add the water, sugar, port and salt. Bring the syrup to a boil over medium heat, stirring until the sugar is dissolved.

3. After the sugar is dissolved, while waiting for the syrup to boil, pack the hot, sterilized jars with plums, divide the orange peel evenly between the jars and put a cinnamon stick in each. Leave ½ inch of space at the top of each jar. This head-space is important to the canning process. When the syrup boils, pour the hot syrup over the plums, filling each jar to within ½ inch of the top, preserving the ½ inch head-space.

4. Use a damp paper towel or cloth to wipe the rim and threads of each jar clean, removing any syrup residue or stickiness. Put the lids on and tighten the rings, then set the jars on the canner rack, adding water if needed to cover the jars by an inch. Bring the All American® to a full boil and keep it there while jars process for 20 minutes. Take the jars out of the canner and set them on a towel or board to cool. Check seals after 24 hours and store in a cool, dark place for up to 1 year.

Honey-Bourbon Pickled Blueberries

Aromatic dessert spices, the rich sweetness only honey can offer, the fruity sweet and tart of blueberries, the tang of the vinegar and the warmth of the bourbon, these flavors and fragrances come together for a taste that is full, layered and complex. Serve Honey-Bourbon Pickled Blueberries with roast pork or atop a creamy, soft goat cheese spread on thinly sliced dark brown bread.

Makes: 6 half-pint jars.

Ingredients:

- 3 inches stick cinnamon
- 1 tsp. whole allspice
- 1 1/4 cups white wine vinegar
- 8 cups blueberries
- 1/4 cup bourbon
- 1 3/4 cups honey

Directions:

1. Put the cinnamon and allspice in the center of a 6-inch square of clean, double layered cheesecloth, then draw up corners. Tie to close creating a spice sachet.

2. Pour vinegar into a large, heavy-bottomed pot. Drop in the spice sachet and bring the vinegar to boiling over medium-high heat. Lower the heat, cover the pot and let it simmer for 5 minutes before adding the blueberries and bourbon.

3. Simmer over medium heat until syrup just heats through, lightly shaking the pot to keep the berries moving. Try not to stir it to avoid breaking berries. This should take about 8 minutes. Turn off the heat and take the pot from the stove. Set it aside, covered, to rest for 8 to 12 hours at room temperature.

4. Fill the All American® with enough water that the full jars will be underneath an inch of water. Bring the water to a boil, then lower the temperature and let it simmer until needed. Wash, rinse and sterilize jars and lids, leaving them in hot water until ready to use.

5. Take the spice sachet out of the pot and discard it. Place a colander over a large bowl and pour the blueberries into it. Keep the liquid. Spoon the hot berries into sterilized hot jars. Make sure to leave a head-space of ½ inch.

6. Put the set aside liquid back into the pot. Add the honey and bring the pot to a boil, stirring often. Let the pot boil, uncovered, until syrup thickens a bit, about 5 minutes. Pour over blueberries, allowing a head-space of ½ inch. With a clean, damp cloth wipe jar rims and threads, then add the lids and rings.

7. Put the jars on the canner rack and bring it to boiling. Hold it there at boiling and process the jars for 10 minutes. Take the jars out of the canner and put them in a safe place to cool.

11

DESSERTS & DELICACIES

PECAN PIE FILLING

Pecans not only make great pies but are great for your health too. I'm a fanatic for pecan pie. This filling is ready to use straight from the jar so just prepare your crust and indulge. Recipe makes 2 quarts.

INGREDIENTS:

- 3 ½ cups pecan halves
- 1 cup light brown sugar
- 4 cups unsweetened apple juice
- ½ tsp. coriander
- ½ tsp. Ginger
- 2 cups sugar
- ½ cup clear jel
- ¼ cup lemon juice
- ½ tsp. cinnamon
- ½ tsp. walnut extract

DIRECTIONS:

1. Combine sugar, spices, walnut extract, apple juice and clear jel in a large pot and heat. Bring to a boil while stirring then add lemon juice and cook for 1 minute. Add pecans and fold to combine.
2. Spoon hot mixture into prepared jars, leaving 1 inch headspace. Remove any air bubbles, wipe the rims of the jars and lids with a clean cloth and fasten lids.
3. Place into the All American® and process for 20 minutes at a full rolling boil.
4. Turn off flame, remove canner cover and allow jars to sit in the pot for a few more minutes. Remove from canner and place on a dish towel and allow to cool undisturbed.

CHERRY PIE FILLING

With this recipe, even on a busy day, there's time for pie. Make a quick crust, pour the filling in and pop it in the oven. Nice and simple, with no artificial colors or flavors to worry about. If sour cherries are not available, you can use sweet cherries. Your filling will be delicious and your pies wonderful with the sweet, but with the sour cherries, they'll be even better. It takes one quart of filling to make a 9-inch pie. This recipe yields 7 quarts of filling, giving you seven delicious, all-but-made cherry pies for your pantry shelf.

INGREDIENTS:

- 6 quarts sour cherries
- 7 cups sugar
- 1 ¾ cups Clear Jel
- 9 cups water
- ½ cup fresh lemon juice

DIRECTIONS:

1. Wash the cherries well, then pat them dry. Remove the pits, working over a bowl so none of the juice is lost. After all of the cherries have been pitted, set the bowl of cherries and cherry juice aside and prepare the canning equipment.
2. Fill your All American® with enough water to cover quart-sized jars by a depth of at least an inch. Bring the water to a boil, then reduce the heat to low to keep the water at a simmer while you work. Thoroughly wash, rinse and sterilize 4 quart jars and their lids, leaving them in simmering water until you're ready to use them.

3. Blanch the cherries by working in batches. Bring a gallon of water to a boil in a large pot. Add about 7-8 cups of cherries at a time. Boil for one minute. This will preserve the flavoring and color of the cherries. Ladle out and place blanched cherries in a colander over a large bowl. This will catch and hold juices as they drip.

4. Mix together the Clear Jel and sugar. Use reserved juice from the bowl and add in enough water to make about 9 cups of liquid. Stir the liquid into the Clear Jel mixture and cook over medium high heat. Stir regularly and wait until mixture begins to thicken. If Clear Jel mixture gets too thick, you can add more water.

5. Stir in the lemon juice and remove from heat. Add the cherries and mix gently.

6. Fill the hot sterilized jars with the hot cherry pie filling, stopping 1 inch from the top of the jar, so you'll have an inch of head-space at the top, under the lid. Carefully wipe the rim and threads of each jar clean with a damp cloth or paper towel. Put on the lids and tighten the rings, then put the jars inside the All American® on the rack.

7. The water in the canner should be deep enough to cover the filled and capped quart jars by an inch. If it isn't, add water until it is as deep as it should be. Bring the water in the canner to a boil. Keep the water boiling and process the jar jars for a full 30 minutes.

8. After the half hour of processing, take the jars out of the canner and set them on a sturdy rack or a clean towel to cool overnight. At the end of 24 hours, check to make sure that each jar sealed as it should have, then store the filling in a dark, cool place for up to 1 year.

SPICED APPLE PIE FILLING

There's nothing quite like the scent of an apple pie wafting through the air. The smell of the apples, sweet and tart, warm and juicy, baking with the cinnamon, nutmeg, ginger and cloves, that is the scent of all good things – holidays, childhood, grandmothers and Sunday dinner desserts. Apple pie just might be the ultimate comfort food. Serve it warm from the oven, with a scoop of ice cream or a dollop or two of whipped cream. Try it with thin slices of extra sharp cheddar cheese. A quart of this filling makes a really nice 9-inch pie. A quart of this spiced apple pie filling also makes a really nice housewarming, hostess, or holiday gift.

Makes: Yields 3 quarts of filling.

INGREDIENTS:

- 10 cups peeled and sliced apples
- 2 ¼ cup apple cider
- 2 cups water
- 6 tbsp. bottled lemon juice
- 1 ½ cups sugar
- ¾ cup Clear Jel
- 1 tbsp. cinnamon
- ¾ tsp. nutmeg
- ½ tsp. ginger
- ¼ tsp. cloves

DIRECTIONS:

1. Blanche the apple slices by dropping them into a large pot of boiling water for 1 minute. Drain away the hot water, then put the apple slices in a bowl with cold water to cover and a little lemon juice. This should offer some protection against discoloration.

2. Prepare your All American®. Fill it with enough water to cover three quart jars by at least an inch. Bring the water to a boil, then lower the heat and keep the water at a gentle simmer. Wash, rinse and sterilize three quart jars and their lids. Leave the jars and lids in simmering water until you are ready to use them.

3. In a large, heavy saucepan, stir the apple cider, water and lemon juice together, then put the pan over medium-high heat. In a medium-sized bowl, use a whisk to blend the sugar, Clear Jel, cinnamon, nutmeg, ginger and cloves.

4. Gradually add the sugar mixture to the cider mixture in the saucepan, whisking all the while to make sure that there are no lumps. Continue using the whisk to stir constantly and bring the mixture in the saucepan to a boil. Let it cook for a few more minutes, stirring constantly, until the mixture begins thickening.

5. When the mixture begins to thicken, gently fold in the apples slices, taking care not to break them, and remove the saucepan from heat. Fill hot, sterile jars with the hot apple pie filling, leaving a full inch of head-space at the top.

6. Wipe the jar rims and threads clean with a damp cloth, then place the jars on the canner rack. Bring the water in the canner to a boil and keep the water boiling while the jars process for 25 minutes.

7. After the processing time is complete, remove the All American® from the hot burner and put it on a cooler burner or a heat resistant trivet on a counter-top or table. Take the cover off of the canner and let the jars sit for another 10 minutes, then take them out and set them on a towel to cool.

8. If the canner, with weight of the water and the jars, is too heavy for you to safely move it without tilting, sloshing or clanking the jars or, worse yet, spilling the scalding hot water on yourself, leave it where it sits. While moving the canner does help some with the cooling and sealing of the jars, it doesn't help enough to make it worth the risk of scalding yourself or losing pie filling to a cracked or broken jar.

9. Let the jars sit undisturbed for 24 hours, then check the seals. If the jars did seal correctly, you can store the pie filling in a dark, cool place for up to a year. If a jar did not seal as it should have, you can store it in the refrigerator, but you'll need to use it within three days.

Mincemeat Pie Filling

Mincemeat is a mixture of fruits and spices that can be used to fill pot pies or even cookies. The Brits are crazy about mincemeat, especially at Christmas (perhaps partly due to the brandy they put in it). The 3 spices of cinnamon, nutmeg and cloves are symbolic of the 3 gifts presented by the wise men to baby Jesus. If you go to London, you'll be sure to see it on restaurant menus. You may use sausage or venison in place of the ground beef. There are sweet and savory flavors blended into this dish. Recipe makes 7 quarts.

Ingredients:

- 2 cups mutton fat (suet), diced
- 5 quarts apples, chopped
- 1 lb. white raisins
- 2 tbsp. ground cinnamon
- 5 cups sugar
- 4 lbs. ground beef
- 2 lbs. seedless dark raisins
- 2 quarts apple cider
- ½ tbsp. of ground nutmeg
- 1 tbsp. ground cloves

2 tbsp. salt

DIRECTIONS:

1. Add beef and suet in a large pot over medium-high heat, pour in ½ cup of water to avoid browning. Stir regularly and cook until the water has evaporated. Peel the apples, remove the cores and cut into cubes. Immediately put into a food processor together with the suet and meat and pulse into a coarse mixture. Return the mixture into the pot, add all remaining ingredients and cook with medium-low heat for 60 minutes or until mixture has thickened. Remove pot from heat.

2. Place hot mixture into prepared jars leaving 1 inch headspace. Remove any air bubbles and wipe the rims of the jars and lids with a clean cloth dampened with vinegar. Close jars as tightly as possible and place them into the prepared pressure canner. Process the filling with a pressure of 10 pounds for 90 minutes.

3. Lower the temperature and let the gauge return to zero. Remove lid from pressure canner and let the jars sit for 10 minutes inside before removing from the pressure canner. Place jars on a clean towel and let them sit overnight undisturbed.

SOUTHEASTERN GREEN TOMATO MINCEMEAT

TWO recipes for Mincemeat???? Guys, trust me, it's that good. This recipe makes 4 quarts of filling, enough for four generously filled pies. That is four fragrant, sweet and spicy pies that can be in the oven in just minutes. To make a pie with this filling, mix enough pastry dough for a single crust pie, roll it out and fit it into the pie pan. Pour in the pie filling and bake at 350 degrees Fahrenheit for 40 to 50 minutes or until the filling is set and a toothpick poked in center of pie comes out clean. If the crust browns too quickly, protect it with foil so it doesn't burn. Serve with lightly sweetened, freshly whipped cream or a scoop of vanilla ice cream.

INGREDIENTS:

- 4 quarts green tomatoes
- 1 ½ lbs. dark brown sugar
- 1 lb. seedless raisins
- 1 tbsp. freshly ground cinnamon
- 1 tbsp. freshly ground nutmeg
- 1 tbsp. salt
- ½ tsp. cloves
- ½ lb. butter
- ¼ cup vinegar

DIRECTIONS:

1. Use a food processor or blender to grind the tomatoes. Drain the juice from the tomatoes and pour it into a measuring cup. If the juice did not reach 2 cups, simply add water to have 2 cups of tomato juice. This is to make sure that the pureed mixture will not burn when simmered.

2. In a large, heavy stainless steel pot, combine tomatoes and the 2 cups of tomato juice. Simmer over medium-low heat until tomatoes are tender and cooked through. Add the rest of the ingredients and simmer for about 2 to 3 hours, or until the mixture has thickened while stirring regularly.
3. While simmering the green tomato mixture, set up the All American® pressure canner and sterilize the jars and lids. Leave the sterile lids and jars in steady simmering water until needed.
4. When the pie filling has thickened, pour the hot filling into sterilized jars, leaving ½ inch of headspace. Wipe jar threads and rims clean with a damp cloth. Put the lids on and tighten the rings. Place them into the prepared pressure canner.
5. Close the lid and process the jars in the All American® pressure canner for 30 minutes at a rolling boil. Make sure water covers the lids of the jars by 1-2 inches and don't start your timer until water has reached a full boil again after adding the jars.
6. When processing is complete, turn off the source of heat. Remove lid and transfer jars to a towel covered area to cool for at least 12 hours, undisturbed and then check jar seals.
7. If jars make a popping sound that means they are cooling and sealing. Check seals and reseal any unsealed jar. Store until needed.

www.ingramcontent.com/pod-product-compliance
Lightning Source LLC
Chambersburg PA
CBHW081346080526
44588CB00016B/2394